Empirical Analysis for Expert Systems

Peter G. Politakis
Digital Equipment Corporation, Hudson, Massachusetts

Empirical Analysis
for Expert Systems

Pitman Advanced Publishing Program

BOSTON · LONDON · MELBOURNE

PITMAN PUBLISHING INC
1020 Plain Street, Marshfield, Massachusetts 02050

PITMAN PUBLISHING LIMITED
128 Long Acre, London WC2E 9AN

Associated Companies
Pitman Publishing Pty Ltd, Melbourne
Pitman Publishing New Zealand Ltd, Wellington
Copp Clark Pitman, Toronto

© Peter G. Politakis 1985

First published 1985

Library of Congress Cataloging in Publication Data

Politakis, Peter G.
  Empirical analysis for expert systems
  Revision of thesis (Ph.D.)—Rutgers University.
  Bibliography: p.
  1. Expert systems (Computer science)   2. System analysis.
  3. SEEK (Computer system)   I. Title
  QA76.76.E95P65   1985   001.64   85-9502
  ISBN 0-273-08663-4

British Library Cataloguing in Publication Data

Politakis, Peter G.
  Empirical analysis for expert systems.
  1. Expert systems (Computer science)
  I. Title
  001.64   QA76.9.E96

  ISBN 0-273-08663-4

Reproduced and printed by photolithography
in Great Britain by Biddles Ltd, Guildford

Contents

Preface

This book describes a system that provides a unified design framework for building and empirically verifying an expert system knowledge base. SEEK is a system which gives interactive advice about rule refinement during the design of an expert system. The advice takes the form of suggestions for possible experiments in generalizing or specializing rules in a model of reasoning rules produced by an expert. Case experience, in the form of stored cases with known conclusions, is used to interactively guide the expert in refining the rules of a model. This approach is most effective when a model of the expert's knowledge is relatively accurate and small changes in the model may improve performance. The system is interactive; we rely on the expert to focus the system on those experiments that appear to be most consistent with his domain knowledge. The design framework of SEEK consists of a tabular model for expressing expert-derived rules and a general consultation system for applying a model to specific cases. The system has been used in building large-scale expert medical consultation systems, with examples taken from an expert consultation model for the diagnosis of rheumatic diseases.

Acknowledgements

This book is a revised version of my Ph.D. dissertation in Computer Science at Rutgers University. I would like to acknowledge the members of my thesis committee. I would like to express my deepest thanks to my supervisor, Professor Sholom Weiss, for his guidance and encouragement. I would like to give thanks to the other members of my committee, Professors Casimir Kulikowski, Tom Mitchell, and Robert Smith. I would also like to thank Professor Saul Amarel for his careful reading and valuable suggestions.

I am indebted to Donald Lindberg, M.D. of the National Library of Medicine, and to Gordon Sharp, M.D., and their fellow researchers at the University of Missouri-Columbia, for their strong support and the contribution of the rheumatological knowledge base.

I would like to acknowledge the support of grant RR-643 from the National Institutes of Health to the Rutgers Laboratory for Computer Science Research.

I am very grateful to the Digital Equipment Corporation and my colleagues in the Artificial Intelligence Applications Group for providing an excellent computing environment during the final preparation of the manuscript.

1. Introduction

1.1 Overview of the Problem

For the past decade, much of the research in the development of expert systems has focused on the acquisition of knowledge for medical diagnosis and treatment. Some of the early prototypical expert systems in medicine included CASNET [47] for ophthalmology, INTERNIST [33] for internal medicine, and MYCIN [36] for infectious diseases. For large systems of this kind, it is well known that better methods for acquiring expert decision-making knowledge are needed to speed up the developmental cycle. Also, the dual problem of how to verify the medical content of an expert system's knowledge base and evaluate its performance is a relatively difficult task especially for the early medical systems where the reasoning strategies were based on rather complex scoring functions to account for the uncertainty in diagnostic tasks.

There have been two approaches to the problem of acquiring expert knowledge. A *direct* approach has tried to find efficient techniques to extract knowledge from the domain expert, while other research efforts have sought ways of acquiring expert knowledge *indirectly* from samples of cases. Key aspects of these approaches are presented in the top two boxes of Figure 1-1. First, we will discuss the direct approach for building an expert medical consultation system.

In general, the work on developing an expert system for medical consultation has relied on the expert physician to provide all the domain-specific knowledge for the system's knowledge base. For instance, the expert specifies the diagnoses that a consultation system is to conclude as well as the relevant findings needed to reach them. Most real-world medical applications are characterized by uncertainty in the clinical diagnoses and a large dimension of the data set which can include hundreds of findings. Because of this and the observation that much of the expert's clinically relevant knowledge is not formally specified but is based on experience, the formalization of decision-making knowledge is well known to be a time-consuming and formidable task in expert system development.

Although production rule representations have been successfully used for expressing expert decision-making knowledge, we still need some framework to facilitate the expert's formulation of rules in the development of an expert system. Finding useful levels of abstraction is a fundamental and difficult part of rule formulation, particularly if we are to

1

reduce a problem's dimensions. The expert physician, like other specialists, does not spend his time writing down his rules of reasoning. Doing such an unaccustomed task as having to explicitly express his rules, the expert has little or no uniform structure to apply in formulating them; he may forget pieces of knowledge, or introduce inconsistencies and mistakes in writing his rules. Despite these practical difficulties, in the past most expert system knowledge bases have been developed in detail before testing is carried out. When empirical evaluation was done, it was limited to a few test cases, with the major goal of verifying performance, rather than as an integral part of the development process.

<table>
<tr><td>

Domain expert derived
Go to the expert for
entire development
of model

Large dimensions

Sometimes tested
with cases

</td><td>

Case derived - samples
Training cases

Relatively small dimensions

Results as good
as case data

</td></tr>
</table>

<table>
<tr><td>

SEEK

Expert-derived Model:
assumed largely correct

Cases to help in rule refinement
and performance analysis

</td></tr>
</table>

Figure 1-1:   Approaches to Building Expert Systems

On the other hand, various methods for acquiring or learning expert rules directly from sample cases have been found to be acceptable if certain characteristics of the domain are known. For example, if the dimensions of the problem area are of manageable size, the features for describing the case data are sufficiently specific for accurate discrimination, and the case data are accurately presented. For limited-sized applications, knowledge that is acquired directly from cases may be adequate for expert decision-making when cases are reasonably representative of the conclusions to be covered. Unfortunately, for most large medical applications, these characteristics usually cannot be met. Even if a large number of cases for a realistic application is available, it is important to note that cases alone do not contain all the domain-specific information which an expert physician can provide to an expert system knowledge base.

Thus the problem consists of a lack of guidance and verification in the development of an expert system knowledge base, since available diagnosed cases may not be sufficient nor reliable enough to be used by themselves. So what can be done? The motivation for this dissertation came from the difficulties that were experienced with previous approaches that relied only on the expert, or those that relied only on samples of cases. While recognizing that the best source of knowledge is the human specialist, the approach described in this book is that the expert's knowledge has to be supplemented by a representative set of cases for *testing* purposes--to be integrated within a unified system that eases the tasks of acquiring and verifying the decision-making knowledge. This approach has been shown to work by the implementation of an interactive system for empirical experimentation with expert knowledge, called SEEK.

1.2 Empirical Analysis in SEEK

SEEK combines design aids for building expert models with empirical testing and evaluation heuristics that help the human specialist carry out experiments to see if he can improve his decision-making knowledge.

SEEK starts with expert-derived rules of inference expressed in a tabular model (a restricted type of production rule system) and uses experience, in the form of stored cases with known conclusions, to interactively guide the expert in refining the rules of a model. Performance information from the cases is integrated into the design process of an expert model by providing advice about rule refinement. SEEK generates advice in the form of suggestions for possible experiments in generalizing or specializing rules in the model. It is the regularities about the performance of rules in misdiagnosed cases that SEEK specifically uses as a basis for suggesting changes to the rules.

Case analysis methods are used to identify slight changes to the rules which may correct the model's results on misdiagnosed cases. Minimal changes are suggested under the assumption that the expert model is generally correct--the expert knows his area and can express his knowledge in the model. This is not to mean that the system will not

3

work when a model is poorly presented. Rather, the system will be most productive in its advice giving when the expert's rules are generally correct and fine-tuning is needed. A summary of these points appears below.

Characteristics of SEEK

Integrates *performance* information into the design cycle of an expert model for diagnostic consultation

Generates *advice* in the form of suggestions for possible *experiments* in *generalizing* or *specializing* rules in an expert model

Looks for *regularities* about the performance of the rules in *misdiagnosed cases* as a basis for suggesting changes to the rules

Uses a *Tabular model* (a restricted production rule system) for the expression of expert-derived rules

Uses *Case experience*, in the form of *stored cases with known conclusions*, to interactively guide the expert in refining the rules of a model

Model is assumed to be basically correct--philosophy on generating *advice* is to suggest *minimal* refinements of the rules

1.3 Outline

The remainder of Chapter 1 provides an overview of the SEEK system that is organized according to certain stages in the development of an expert model. The tabular model for representing expert knowledge is described and a summary of the model refinement process is presented. Examples are given from an expert model for diagnosing rheumatic diseases.

Chapter 2 reviews related research on knowledge acquisition and expert system development and evaluation.

Chapter 3 describes the methods by which performance statistics are gathered from the model's past experience in diagnosing cases. The central component in gathering performance statistics is the application of case analysis methods on each misdiagnosed case.

4

The methods of case analysis identify rules for refinement such that a misdiagnosed case may be correctly diagnosed by the model when these rules are modified. Many examples are presented to illustrate the application of these case analysis methods. Gathering performance statistics represents the first of a two-step process in the generation of advice about rule refinement.

Chapter 4 describes heuristics for proposing rule refinement experiments. The heuristics relate certain statistics about a rule's past performance on a data base of cases to determine modifications of the rules in an expert model. The process of interpreting the heuristics constitutes the second step for the automatic generation of advice about rule refinement. Several examples are included to facilitate the description of the heuristics.

Chapter 5 provides an annotated sample session with SEEK. Many of the system's interactive facilities are demonstrated in the course of refining rules to find an improved formulation of the model.

Chapter 6 reviews the main points of this research, and makes several suggestions for future work.

1.4 Overview of SEEK

This book describes an interactive program called SEEK that is an attempt to unify certain parts of the knowledge acquisition and validation processes into a single design framework. SEEK requires two knowledge sources: the domain expert's knowledge, represented by expert-derived rules, and case experience, in the form of a data base of cases with known diagnostic conclusions. SEEK integrates performance information into the design of an expert system to facilitate the process of experimenting with possible rule changes. A set of domain independent heuristics generate advice about rule refinement by looking for regularities about the performance of the rules on misdiagnosed cases.

1.5 The Model

A table of criteria, which is a specialized type of frame or prototype [1], is prepared for each potential diagnosis. The table consists of two parts:

- major and minor observations which are significant for reaching the diagnosis,

- a set of diagnostic rules for reaching the diagnosis.

Figure 1-2 shows observations, grouped under the headings *Major* and *Minor* for mixed connective tissue disease. For this disease, there are five major observations that the expert considers very important, while the six minors such as *mild Myositis* are less specific but suggestive of the disease.

Major Criteria	Minor Criteria
1. Swollen hands	1. Myositis, mild
2. Sclerodactyly	2. Anemia
3. Raynaud's phenomenon or esophageal hypomotility	3. Pericarditis
4. Myositis, severe	4. Arthritis $<=$ 6 wks
5. CO diff capacity, nl: < 70	5. Pleuritis
	6. Alopecia

Figure 1-2: Example of Major and Minor findings

The second part of the table contains the diagnostic rules. In Figure 1-3, each column consists of a rule for a specific degree of certainty in the diagnosis. There are three levels of confidence: *possible, probable* or *definite*. A diagnostic rule is a conjunction of three components which are taken from the rows: specific numbers of majors or minor observations, requirements, and exclusions. Requirements are those combinations of observations which are necessary beyond simple numbers of major and minor findings (although major and minor findings also may be requirements). Exclusions are those observations which rule out the diagnosis at the indicated confidence level. The three fixed confidence levels are an important attribute of the model. They substitute for complex scoring functions which can be a major difficulty in analyzing and explaining model performance [41]. It is understood that the rule with the strongest confidence level for a given diagnosis supersedes those with lower confidence. For example, if a definite diagnosis for a particular disease is made, even if the rules for the probable or possible diagnosis for the same disease are satisfied, the definite conclusion is considered more appropriate.

	Definite	Probable	Possible
	4 majors	2 majors 2 minors	3 majors
Requirements	Positive RNP antibody	Positive RNP antibody	No requirement
Exclusions	Positive SM antibody	No exclusion	No exclusion

Figure 1-3: Tabular Format for the Expert's Rules

As an example, the rule for concluding definite mixed connective tissue disease can be stated as follows: If the patient has 4 or more Major observations for mixed connective tissue disease, and RNP antibody is positive, and SM antibody is not positive, then conclude definite mixed connective tissue disease. In most applications, multiple rules are described for each confidence level. Furthermore, the components of the tabular model rules are not restricted only to observations which are asked during a consultation session. There may be intermediate results obtained by reasoning rules expressed in other tables; for example, the minor labeled *Pleuritis* in Figure 1-2 may be derived by rules in a tabular model for reaching this conclusion. A more detailed analysis of the model structure is presented in Chapter 3, and examples of the tabular model format are shown in Appendix II.

The following sections will focus on tools for model refinement that aid in identifying two classes of changes which can be made to the rules: *generalizations* or *specializations*. Generalizations are changes that weaken a rule R, resulting in a different rule R_g where R_g logically includes R. For example, this can be accomplished by dropping a requirement or decreasing the number of major and minor findings for a rule. Specializations are changes that strengthen a rule R, resulting in a different rule R_s where R_s is logically included by R; for example, increasing the number of major and minor findings in a rule.

Frame-like schemes have been used to represent medical knowledge in the PIP [30] and CENTAUR [2] systems which were designed to provide diagnostic consultations in subspecialties of medicine. In addition to representing various clinical states, with expected ranges of measurements, and related diseases in each disease frame, those frames contained slots containing relatively complex scoring functions that could be specialized for the evaluation of the disease frame. The tabular model presented here is a simple type of frame representation requiring fixed types of observations (e.g., majors, exclusions) for each diagnostic conclusion that are relatively easy to describe. Scoring follows directly from the three confidence levels of *definite, probable,* and *possible.*

1.6 The Rheumatology Application

A consultation model for connective tissue diseases has been developed using the EXPERT system [46] for developing consultation models. This project is a collaborative effort between researchers at Rutgers University and the University of Missouri. The connective tissue diseases subset of rheumatic diseases are particularly difficult to diagnose.

They include the following seven diseases: rheumatoid arthritis, systemic lupus erythematosus (SLE), progressive systemic sclerosis, mixed connective tissue disease, polymyositis, primary Raynaud's syndrome, and Sjogren's disease. Some of the difficulties in the differential diagnosis of these diseases may be appreciated by noting that that the disease process evolves in atypical ways, that there is a general lack of deterministic criteria to objectively confirm diagnoses, and that even the experts in this area disagree about some of the diagnoses [24].

A key design strategy for building the rheumatology model has been the testing of the model against a data base of clinical cases. The correct diagnosis for each case was decided by agreement of at least two out of three rheumatologists. After an initial design consisting of 18 observations and 35 rules, the model has undergone many cycles of testing and revision. This incremental process resulted in the expansion of the model to include 150 observations, of which several observations were combined by rules to reach intermediate conclusions, and a total of 147 rules. The model has been critiqued by an external panel of expert rheumatologists, and a review of performance has shown the model to achieve diagnostic accuracy in 94% of 145 clinical cases [24]. Current efforts include expanding the model to cover other rheumatic diseases and to provide advice about treatment management. At this time, the dimensions of the model include 30 final diagnostic conclusions, 600 intermediate conclusions, 900 observations, and over 1000 production rules.

1.7 Stages of Model Development

To perform the empirical analysis, SEEK must have a tabular model for each final diagnosis. Also required is a data base of cases, including the correct final diagnosis assigned to each case. The design of a model and the analysis of performance can be segmented into the following steps:

- Initial design of the model

- Data entry: cases and expert's conclusions

- Performance analysis of the model

- Generation of model refinement experiments

- Impact of model changes on the data

Figure 1-4 illustrates the relationships between components of the SEEK system that involve the above steps.

1.8 Initial Design of the Model

A specialized text editor is used to specify an initial design of the model. The EMACS editor [38] has been extended with commands tailored to the tabular model structure. Either one of three editing modes can be specified by the model designer: table input, table update, or table review and store. For each newly identified final diagnosis, *table input* mode allows the model designer to list major and minor observations and to specify components of the rules that would conclude the diagnosis. In *update mode,* the table for a specified final diagnosis is retrieved and the model designer can revise the rules or the lists of major and minor observations. When the additions and updates are completed, the table is stored and translated into a format used by SEEK. The translation of the table format is compatible with the EXPERT system format [46] (Refer to Appendix II for examples of the formats involved.)

1.9 Entry of Data in a Consultation Session

SEEK analyzes the performance of a model's conclusions; it does not attempt to analyze the performance of a questioning strategy. Although SEEK appears to be a separate program, a consultation session is actually run by EXPERT as a subprocess of SEEK. Therefore, the consultation session itself is identical to that produced by EXPERT. In this section we will briefly illustrate a consultation session for the rheumatology model. However, the form of questioning is quite similar to many other medical consultation systems which have been reviewed elsewhere (e.g., [47].)

A questionnaire is used to enter the observations, including the correct presumptive diagnosis for a case. Editing facilities are available to review and to change the responses to questions. A case is stored in a data base which is maintained by the system. The following highly abstracted example shows the typical entry of data for a particular case where the user's responses appear in **boldface**.

9

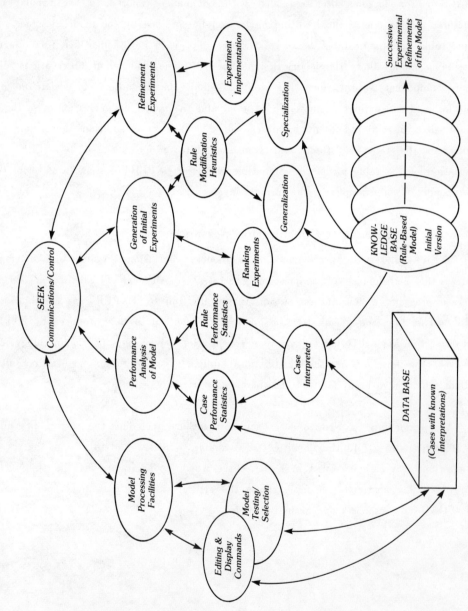

Figure 1-4: Stages of Model Design and Analysis in SEEK

.
.
.

3. Extremity Findings:
    1) Arthralgia
    2) Arthritis <=6 wks, or non-polyarticular
    3) Chronic polyarthritis >6 wks.
    4) Erosive arthritis
    5) Deformity: subluxations or contractures
    6) Swollen hands, observed
    7) Raynaud's phenomenon
    8) Polymyalgia syndrome
    9) Synovial fluid inflammatory
   10) Subcutaneous nodules
   Checklist:
   *1,2,3,4,10

.
.
.

31. Presumptive Diagnosis:
    1) Mixed Connective Tissue Disease
    2) Rheumatoid Arthritis
    3) Systemic Lupus Erythematosus
    4) Progressive Systemic Sclerosis
    5) Polymyositis
    6) Primary Raynaud's
    7) Sjogren's
   Checklist:
   *2

After all questions have been asked, the system provides a summary of the data in the case. From this, the expert can correct any data entry errors and later, the case can be stored in a data base. Cases are usually entered in large groups during a single session. The cycle is repeated for each case: the data are entered, errors are corrected, and the case is saved. An example of the interpretative analysis of the rheumatology model is shown in Figure 1-5. This format, designed by our collaborators at the University of Missouri, has proven very satisfactory in the rheumatology consultation system. Similar formats for diagnostic descriptions can be used in other applications.

The sample interpretation includes the differential diagnosis (i.e., definite rheumatoid arthritis and possible SLE) followed by detailed lists of supporting and conflicting findings which provide a more complete picture of the case. These lists are obtained by matching findings from the case data to prespecified lists that are associated with each diagnosis in the model. The lists include those findings that are consistent, not expected, and unknown for the diagnosis.

INTERPRETIVE ANALYSIS

Diagnoses are considered in the categories
definite, probable, and possible.

Based on the information provided,
the differential diagnosis is

Rheumatoid arthritis (RA)   --   Definite

Systemic lupus erythematosus (SLE)   --   Possible

Patient findings consistent with RA:
   Chronic polyarthritis >6 wks.
   RA factor (l.f.), titer 1: < 320
   Subcutaneous nodules
   Erosive arthritis

Patient findings not expected with RA:
   Oral/nasal mucosal ulcers

Patient findings consistent with SLE:
   Platelet count, /cmm: <= 99999
   Oral/nasal mucosal ulcers
   Arthritis <=6 wks, or non-polyarticular

Patient findings not expected with SLE:
   Erosive arthritis

Unknown findings which would support the diagnosis of SLE:
   LE cells
   DNA antibody (hem.)
   DNA antibody (CIEP)
   DNA (hem.), titer 1:
   FANA
   Sm antibody (imm.)

End of diagnostic consultation: 29-Jul-82.

Figure 1-5:   Sample Diagnostic Interpretation

1.10 Model Performance

A typical interaction with SEEK involves iterating through these steps:

1. obtain performance of rules on the stored cases,

2. analyze the rules,

3. revise the rules.

In reviewing the performance of a model, the expert's conclusions are matched to the model's conclusions. The expert's conclusion is stored with each case, while the model's conclusion is taken as that conclusion reached with the greatest certainty. Figure 1-6 illustates the process of generating experiments for a model.

1.10.1 Conditions for Performance Evaluation

The first step in an analysis of performance is to produce a performance summary for all stored cases. Performance is evaluated by matching the expert's conclusion to the model's conclusion in each case. A practical problem for scoring the results in a particular case occurs when ties in certainty between the expert's conclusion and the model's different conclusion are noted. Whether the model is scored as correct or incorrect for such a case affects the direction of subsequent rule refinements. A decision on how ties should be treated in performance evaluation rests with the problem domain. Whereas ties may be acceptable in particular medical areas for which it is difficult to discriminate between competing diagnoses, they probably would not be acceptable in areas for which the diagnostic choices are well understood and mutually exclusive. Rheumatology is an area that exemplifies the former condition. For instance, some rheumatic diseases do coexist during the progression of the respective disease processes and therefore a final diagnosis is difficult to make. In such cases, a tentative diagnosis may be made while not ruling out other related diseases. An interpretation of a model's conclusions could reflect this situation by treating ties in certainty to be correct (e.g., ties in certainty at the possible or probable confidence level). There may be exceptions. For example, ties at the definite level and at the null level (i.e., no conclusion was reached by the model) may be considered incorrect for diagnostically related diseases. Thus there is a need to specify conditions under which performance evaluation is to be performed. SEEK allows the model designer to specify how ties in confidence are to be treated.

Another analysis condition is to allow the model designer to determine which rules

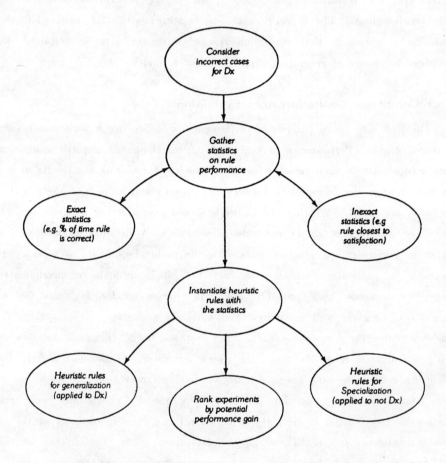

Figure 1-6: Overview of the Process of Generating Experiments

and cases are to be ignored during the evaluation process. This is useful when either there are insufficient numbers of cases for a particular final diagnosis, or the rules for some diagnoses are not deemed to be in a satisfactory state by the model designer. If not ignored, these rules usually interfere in several case diagnoses and their performance over all cases is therefore quite low. SEEK allows the model designer to specify rules to be ignored during performance evaluation and also cases where, for example, rules are deemed "solid".

1.10.2 Performance Summary for the Model

The results are organized according to final conclusions and show the number of cases in which the model's conclusion matches the expert's conclusion (refer to Figure 1-7 below.) The column labeled False Positives shows the number of cases in which the indicated conclusion was reached by the model but did not match the stored expert's conclusion. In Figure 1-7, the summary of performance for mixed connective tissue disease indicates that 9 cases out of 33 were correctly diagnosed. Furthermore, there are no cases which were misdiagnosed by the model as mixed connective tissue disease. The rules that conclude rheumatoid arthritis perform quite well for the stored rheumatoid arthritis cases, but they appear to be candidates for specialization, because of the 10 false positives.

	True Positives		False Positives	
Mixed Connective Tissue Disease	9/ 33	(27%)	0	(00%)
Rheumatoid Arthritis	42/ 42	(100%)	10	(13%)
Systemic Lupus Erythematosus	12/ 18	(67%)	4	(04%)
Progressive Systemic Sclerosis	22/ 23	(96%)	5	(04%)
Polymyositis	4/ 5	(80%)	1	(01%)
Total	89/121	(74%)		

Figure 1-7: Summary of Current Performance

In addition to the results shown in Figure 1-7, general performance results about a specific rule can be obtained, showing the number of cases in which the rule was satisfied. An example of this is shown in Figure 1-8. This summary of a rule's performance includes the number of cases in which the rule was used successfully (i.e., matching the expert's conclusions stored with the cases) and the number of cases in which the rule was used incorrectly (i.e., not matching the expert's conclusions stored with the cases).

Rule 72:   2 or more Majors for RA
            2 or more Minors for RA
            No Exclusion for RA
            → Probable Rheumatoid arthritis

43 Cases: in which this rule was satisfied.
13 Cases: in which the greatest certainty in a conclusion was obtained
            by this rule and it matched the expert's conclusion.
7 Cases: in which the greatest certainty in a conclusion was obtained
            by this rule and it did not match the expert's conclusion.

Figure 1-8:   Summary of Rule Performance

1.11 Analysis of the Model

Interactive assistance for rule refinement is provided during the analysis of the model. The model designer has the option of analyzing either a *single case* or *all cases* to obtain improvements in rule performance.

1.11.1 Analysis of the Model for a Single Case

The objective of single case analysis is to provide the model designer with an explanation of the model's results for that case. By seeing how the model performed on a single case, the model designer can at least verify that the case data had been entered correctly. In fact, this has been a primary use of single case analysis in the rheumatology application where hundreds of findings may be available for a patient case. In section 1.12 we describe how this information presented in single case analysis is gathered and used by SEEK for automatically generating experiments to refine the rules.

Single case analysis is accomplished by first showing the model's confidence in both the expert's conclusion and the model's conclusion. Rules are cited which were used to reach these conclusions. Rules for the expert's conclusion are selected from those rules in the model with the same conclusion as the conclusion stored with the case. If the model's conclusion does not match the expert's conclusion in the case, the system attempts to locate a partially satisfied rule for the expert's conclusion that is the *closest* to being satisfied and would override the model's incorrect conclusion. A procedure for finding the closest rule is described later. An example of the results of single case analysis is shown below. The case in Figure 1-9 is misdiagnosed by the model, which has assigned the certainty value of *possible* to progressive systemic sclerosis. The model's conclusion is rheumatoid arthritis with a certainty value of *probable*. Rule 111 and rule 72 are responsible for reaching these conclusions at the indicated certainty levels. In this example

16

1. *Expert's* conclusion: Progressive systemic sclerosis

2. *Model's* conclusion: Probable rheumatoid arthritis

Strongest satisfied rule for the expert's conclusion:

> rule 111:   1 or more majors for pss   (1 majors satisfied)
>   1 or more minors for pss   (3 minors satisfied)
>
>   → Possible progressive systemic sclerosis

Rule for the model's conclusion:

> rule 72:   2 or more majors for ra   (2 majors satisfied)
>   2 or more minors for ra   (3 minors satisfied)
>   no exclusion for ra   (satisfied)
>
>   → Probable rheumatoid arthritis

Rules for expert's conclusion with potential weight greater than or equal to the model's conclusion:

> rule 112:   requirement 1 for probable pss   (not set)
>   no exclusion for probable pss   (satisfied)
>
>   → Probable progressive systemic sclerosis

Figure 1-9:   Analyzing a Misdiagnosed Case

rule 72 was triggered because 2 majors and 3 minors for rheumatoid arthritis are present and this case did not have the (exclusion) findings that would deny rule 72. Given this information the model designer can pursue either of two directions to refine the rules: either to weaken rule 72 so that it will not override rule 111, or to find a stronger rule concluding progressive systemic sclerosis. In response to this latter possibility, SEEK cites rule 112 as a likely candidate to generalize. A procedure that SEEK uses to identify rules such as rule 112 is described later.

Besides this information provided in single case analysis, SEEK allows the model designer to interrogate any conclusion in the model, both final and intermediate results. The rules for any conclusion can be cited by specifying a rule number or the internal label tagged to a conclusion (e.g., PSS for Progressive systemic sclerosis). If desired, these labels can be displayed with the rules. All rules for a conclusion can be cited, both totally satisfied and partially satisfied rules in the case. This aids the model designer in reviewing the performance of a subset of the rules on the case data.

1.11.2 Analysis of the Model based on Multiple Case Experience

After the performance summary is obtained (Figure 1-7), a global analysis of the model may be tried. The first step in the analysis of a model based on multiple case experience is to specify a final diagnosis for which rules are to be analyzed. In this manner, the model designer focuses the analysis on a subset of the rules in the model. The analysis is usually done after performance results for all diagnoses have been obtained. SEEK assists the model designer in the analysis of a subset of the rules which are relevant to the misdiagnosed cases. An important design consideration for SEEK is to provide the model designer with a flexible means to perform experiments in refining the rules. In this section, advice will be described which helps in determining the specific experiments for rule refinement. Heuristic procedures are needed to select experiments from the many possibilities. For example, SEEK uses a heuristic procedure to determine the rules that agree with the expert's conclusion which are closest to being satisfied in a misdiagnosed case. It looks for a partially satisfied rule in a case for which the following conditions hold:

1. The rule concludes at a minimum confidence level which is greater than (or equal to, depending on the treatment of ties) the certainty value for the model's conclusion;

2. The rule contains the maximum number of satisfied components for all rules concluding at that confidence level.

A rule satisfying these conditions is marked for generalization (weakening), so that it may be invoked more frequently. The rule used to reach the model's conclusion is marked for specialization (strengthening), so that it may be invoked less frequently. A more detailed discussion of the heuristic rules is given in section 1.12.

After analysis of the rules for a given conclusion, SEEK reports the results by numbering and listing rules that are potential candidates for generalization or specialization. Figure 1-10 shows a summary of this rule analysis and includes unsatisfied rules in the misdiagnosed cases that are candidate rules for generalization. The column labeled *Generalization* stands for the number of cases suggesting the generalization of a rule, and the column labeled *Specialization* stands for the number of cases suggesting the specialization of a rule.

In Figure 1-10, rules at the possible level of certainty are strong candidates for generalization. Although Rule 56 is not satisfied in 8 misdiagnosed cases, if Rule 56 ha

Mixed Connective Tissue Disease

Rule	Certainty	Generalization	Specialization
54.	Possible	2	0
55.	Possible	7	0
56.	Possible	8	0
57.	Probable	2	0
58.	Probable	2	0

Figure 1-10: Summary of Preditive Statistics for MCTD Rules

been satisfied these 8 cases would have been correctly diagnosed. In the 8 cases cited for Rule 56, Rule 56 is closer to being satisfied than Rule 55 and all the other rules. A more detailed analysis of each rule, summarizing the satisfied and unsatisfied components of the rule, is normally obtained at this point. Rule 55 can be stated as: If the patient has 2 or more Major observations for mixed connective tissue disease and RNP antibody is positive, then conclude possible mixed connective tissue disease. Rule 56 can be stated as: If the patient has 3 or more Major observations for mixed connective tissue disease, then conclude possible mixed connective tissue disease. A simple experiment for generalization of Rule 56, which might be tried first because it is the simpler rule, is to decrease the number of major observations that it requires.

1.12 Overview of Model Refinement

This section summarizes how advice about refinements to a model's rules can be automatically generated based on an empirical performance analysis of the rules. If we ignore for the moment the possibility of changing the confidence for a rule, a rule can be changed in one of two ways. One can *weaken* the conditions in a rule by removing components in the antecedent and thereby make the rule easier to satisfy. This is called a generalization of the rule. Alternatively, a rule's conditions can be *strengthened* by adding components. This is called a specialization of the rule and would make the rule more difficult to satisfy. The advice generated by the system consists of specific generalizations and specializations of the rules in a model. These are presented in the form of proposed experiments from which the model designer can choose to subsequently try so that he may improve the model's performance on a data base of cases.

Changing a rule's confidence can be viewed as a generalization or a specialization of

19

the rule. Increasing a rule's confidence falls in the category of generalizations because the impact of the rule would be weighted more heavily over the same rule which had lower assigned confidence. Similarly, decreasing a rule's confidence reduces the impact of the rule since the rule would be weighted less. This is in the class of specializations. We discuss next the task of generating rule refinement experiments. Figure 1-11 exemplifies the process of analyzing and recommending rule change experiments for hypothetical diagnosis DX2. In this example, the results of the model and the expert do not match for case 2. Because DX2 is the correct answer for case 2, performance might be improved by generalizing a DX2 rule or specializing a DX1 rule.

1.12.1 Heuristics for Suggesting Experiments

Heuristics are needed to suggest specific rule refinement experiments from the many possibilities that could be tried to correct misdiagnosed cases. Unlike the example in Figure 1-10, situations often arise where some empirical evidence supports the generalization and other evidence supports the specialization of the same rule. In one misdiagnosed case, a satisfied rule could have been found to be responsible for incorrectly diagnosing the case. On the other hand, the same rule could have been unsatisfied in several other misdiagnosed cases where, if it were satisfied, the rule could have correctly diagnosed these cases.

Given this situation, one would reasonably focus on ways to weaken the rule as opposed to strengthening the rule because the empirical evidence favors this approach. Thus a generalization experiment would be needed so that the rule will be satisfied in the subset of misdiagnosed cases for which this rule should be applied. The heuristics must therefore contain information about a rule's performance in order to determine whether to weaken or to strengthen a rule. Furthermore, other empirical information is needed to select a specific experiment. In the case of a generalization experiment, there must be a way of determining the specific component(s) that ought to be removed from the rule. This means that we need to gather statistics about a rule's performance on a data base of cases.

Statistics about a rule's performance on the entire data base of cases enter in heuristic rules to determine rule refinement experiments. Each heuristic rule uses these statistics to help determine:

1. the class of experiment (generalization or specialization) to be suggested;

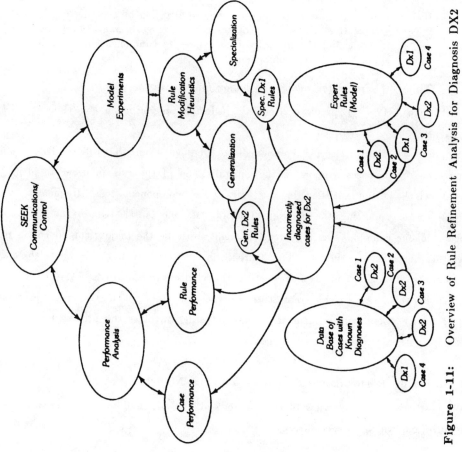

Figure 1-11: Overview of Rule Refinement Analysis for Diagnosis DX2

21

2. the specific component to change in the rule.

In Figure 1-12, an example of a heuristic rule is shown for suggesting an experiment that decreases the number of majors in a rule.

There are two points to note about this heuristic. First, this experiment is in the class of generalizations, so we must verify that a generalization of the rule is needed. This condition is expressed in the first clause of the heuristic. It requires that the number of cases suggesting generalization of the rule exceeds that for specialization of the rule.

> **If:** the number of cases suggesting generalization of the rule is greater than the number of cases suggesting specialization of the rule and the most frequently missing component in the rule is the "MAJOR" component,

> **Then:** *Decrease the number of major findings in the rule.*

Figure 1-12: Example of Heuristic Rule for Suggesting an Experiment

Secondly, we must select a component to remove from the rule. This requires searching each of the cases supporting the generalization of the rule in order to identify a component which is not satisfied in the rule. The component most frequently missed among the cases supporting the generalization of the rule is selected as the item to be weakened. In our example, this missing component must be the majors component in order to suggest the specific experiment. The heuristic is evaluated by filling in the clauses with the appropriate statistics and testing whether the clauses are satisfied. All heuristics are interpreted in this way. This represents the second stage of a two-stage process in generating advice about rule refinement. The first stage involves the process by which the statistics are gathered and is described next.

1.12.2 Gathering Performance Statistics about a Model

We now present an overview of the methods of analysis used to determine which rule to generalize and which to specialize.

Given a case that is misdiagnosed by the model, SEEK performs an analysis on the rules that reach the expert's conclusion. As an example, let the expert's conclusion be denoted by the symbol E and the model's different and therefore incorrect conclusion be identified by the symbol M. Suppose the model's confidence in the expert's conclusion E possible, while the model's confidence in M is *probable*. The two rules responsible for reaching these conclusions are R_e for the expert's conclusion and R_m for the model's conclusion. This is described in Figure 1-13.

	Conclusion	Rule responsible
Model's confidence in the Expert's conclusion:	possible E	R_e
Model's conclusion:	probable M	R_m

Figure 1-13: Summary Information about a Misdiagnosed Case

1.12.2.1 Generalization Statistics

Since the model concludes for the expert's conclusion *possible* E and the model's conclusion is *probable* M, we need to find a *stronger* rule for E in order to override the model's incorrect conclusion. We need to find a rule for the expert's conclusion E with confidence that is at least *probable*. (We assume for all examples that ties in confidence between the expert's conclusion and the model's conclusion are acceptable, and therefore when they occur, the model is to be scored as correctly diagnosing such a case.) Since no rule was satisfied that concludes the expert's conclusion E with confidence greater than *possible*, we could try to find a candidate rule to generalize which is *partially satisfied*. A simple example of a partially satisfied rule is a rule which needs at least 2 major findings, but only one major finding is satisfied. As an alternative to finding a partially satisfied rule to generalize, we could change the confidence of rule R_e from *possible* to *probable*.

While this latter change is simple to perform, it is quite drastic. This can be understood by examining how a model is prepared. Rules are written with specific levels of confidence in mind. Changing a rule's confidence would mean that the whole rule is in error and not just a component in the rule. When a rule is *moved* from one confidence level to another (e.g., from possible to probable) the expert's expectation in the importance of the rule is altered relative to all rules for a specific diagnosis. Although the system generates experiments for changing a rule's confidence, we are more interested in determining changes that are less radical, and comprise more subtle variations in the expert's rules.

We may be able to correct the case by changing rules for the expert's conclusion. Several rules are usually applicable for generalization, each of which can be weakened in many ways. We want to select a rule which would correct the case, with as little modification as possible to achieve this. A predictive statistic is needed to identify a rule such that if the rule were satisfied, it would correct the case and secondly, that it should be the *closest* to being satisfied among all applicable rules. We describe below a process by which this statistic is gathered for each misdiagnosed case. This is different from a statistic that simply logs what happened in each case, for example, whether a particular rule was satisfied in the case.

For each of the partially satisfied rules found for the expert's conclusion E, a backtracing procedure is performed on the components in the left-hand side of the rule to obtain a measure of the percentage of total satisfaction. A component in a rule may itself have rules which conclude it, requiring additional backtracing over such rules; in an advanced version of a rheumatology model, there are as many as six levels of rules. This procedure involves counting the number of components in a rule *needed* for satisfaction and the number of components actually *satisfied* by the case data. Intuitively, the idea is to select a rule to generalize which is the *closest* to being satisfied, and it concludes with minimal confidence needed to correct the case.

A partially satisfied rule for the expert's conclusion E is selected that has the greatest percentage of total satisfaction; call this rule R_e'. The *first* unsatisfied component found in this rule R_e' is identified to be weakened. The result of this analysis means that if rule R_e' was satisfied, the case would then be correctly diagnosed. Rule R_e' would override the model's incorrect conclusion of M caused by rule R_m. Further, the rule R_e' would be easier to satisfy if the first unsatisfied component found in the rule was removed. This summarizes the analysis to select a candidate rule for generalizaton of the expert's conclusion. This analysis is performed on each misdiagnosed case, and the summed statistics for candidate rules to generalize are recorded for subsequent use by the heuristics.

1.12.2.2 Specialization Statistics

In addition to gathering statistics about rules to generalize, we also carry out a analysis of the rules yielding incorrect conclusions for a misdiagnosed case, so as to collec information about *strengthening* the conditions of these rules. By definition, a case i misdiagnosed by the model when the model's strongest conclusion does not match th expert's conclusion stored in the case. To determine candidate rules to specialize, we nee to identify all conclusions reached by the model which override the model's confidence i the expert's conclusion. A problem with determining specialization experiments is that

24

single rule change is often not enough to correct the case. It is not uncommon to find multiple problems with the rules because more than one conclusion was reached with a confidence level exceeding that of the expert's conclusion.

Because of this we separate our conclusions into two classes of specialization: *primary* and *secondary* specialization. Primary specialization contains only the model's incorrect conclusion which was reached with greatest certainty among all conclusions. The class called secondary specialization contains all other incorrect conclusions.

For each incorrect case, the rules that reach the *primary* specialization conclusion are traced. The results of this trace on each rule are used to determine the effect of specializing the rule on the performance of the case. That is, if we force the rule not to be satisfied, then how *close* is the case to being correctly diagnosed?

In our example, the rules that conclude M are the subject of this analysis. Rule R_m was responsible for reaching the conclusion of *probable* M. This rule should not have been invoked, and therefore it is identified to be a candidate for primary specialization. If conclusions other than M were reached in the case with confidence exceeding possible E, then the rules that reach these conclusions would be identified for secondary specialization. A measure of closeness to correcting the case if rule R_m is not satisfied is associated with this rule. This measure is derived from the number of satisfied rules for M and the number of conclusions in the secondary class of specialization. This summarizes the rule analysis leading to the specialization of rules. The statistics are recorded for each misdiagnosed case and made available to evaluate the heuristics.

The statistics for primary and secondary specialization are not enough to determine a specific experiment. For instance, information about which component to add to a rule is not readily obtained for a specialization experiment as it is for generalization (to determine a component to remove from a rule). Knowledge of the types of components (e.g., majors, minors, requirements) that can appear in a rule can help us to focus on a component to be specialized. The heuristics for suggesting specialization experiments can include a preference in changing one component over another, based on an intuitive understanding of the components in the tabular model.

Given a tabular model for a conclusion, one preferred ordering for changing components in the rules expressed in this model could be: minors are preferred over majors, and majors are preferred over requirements. As an example, if a rule that is identified for specialization expresses a number of minors and a number of majors, then according to the preference ordering one would strengthen the minors component.

Frequency data about a component on the entire data base of cases is another source of information that is useful to determine a component to add to a rule; but the best source of information for adding a component is the expert.

1.12.3 Summary of Model Refinement Advice

In summary, the generation of advice about changes to a model is a two-stage process. The first stage involves gathering statistics about rule performance as a result of analyzing all cases in the data base. The second stage is the evaluation of the heuristic rules using the statistics showing the rules' performance, for the purpose of suggesting specific experiments about rule refinement. The potential loss as a result of generalizing a rule by either removing a component or increasing the confidence is the increase in the number of false positives already attributed to the rule. In Figure 1-13, a generalization experiment could have an adverse effect on the performance of correct cases where the expert's conclusions is other than conclusion E. On the other hand, the potential loss as a result of specializing a rule by either adding a component or decreasing the confidence is the decrease in the number of cases in which the rule was significant in reaching the correct conclusion. The exact impact of a change is ascertained by trying an experiment that conditionally incorporates a change into the model and tests the model on the data base of cases.

1.13 Generation of Model Refinement Experiments

As was shown in Figure 1-10, SEEK indicated several rules that were candidates for generalization. In general, there are many possibilities that can be tried for refining the rules in a model. A heuristic rule-based scheme is used to suggest experiments. The IF part of the heuristic rule contains a conjunction of predicate clauses that looks for certain features about the performance of rules in the model while the THEN part of the heuristic rule contains a specific rule refinement experiment. An example of a heuristic rule was shown in Figure 1-12 and was used to suggest the specific generalization experiment to decrease the number of major findings in a rule. Currently, there are about a dozen heuristic rules which are divided almost equally with respect to the types of experiment (i.e., generalizations or specializations) that may be suggested.

Evaluation of a heuristic rule begins by instantiating the clauses with the required empirical information about a specific rule in the model. Function calls are used to gather the information. After instantiation, the clauses are evaluated in order, beginning with the first clause in the heuristic rule. If all clauses are satisfied, then the specific experiment is posted. All heuristic rules are evaluated in this manner for a specific rule in the model. The experiments suggested by the heuristic rules are narrowed by the expert to those changes consistent with his medical knowledge. In Figure 1-14, the experiments suggested for the rules used in reaching the diagnosis of mixed connective tissue disease are presented after listing the misdiagnosed mixed connective tissue disease cases.

24 cases in which the expert's conclusion MCTD does not match the model's conclusion:

1, 4, 11, 12, 14, 15, 42, 47, 49, 57, 60, 67, 71, 75, 78, 80, 84, 93, 99, 100, 104, 105, 107, 130,

Proposed Experiments for Mixed Connective Tissue Disease

1. Decrease the number of majors in rule 56.

2. Delete the requirement component in rule 55.

3. Delete the requirement component in rule 54.

4. Decrease the number of minors in rule 57.

5. Delete the requirement component in rule 58.

Figure 1-14: Example of Suggested Experiments for Rule Refinement

The experiments are ordered based on maximum potential performance gain. Other criteria for ordering can be used such as ease of change, such as an experiment that suggests a change in the minors of a rule might be preferred over an experiment to change the majors. An explanation of a particular experiment is provided by a translation of the specific heuristic rule used to suggest the experiment into a narrative statement containing the empirical information about the rule. In Figure 1-15, the support for the first experiment is given. It should be emphasized that a decision as to which experiments are to be tried, if any, is left to the model designer. Even though a particular experiment is supported empirically, an experiment must be justified in terms of other knowledge about the domain. For example, is a rule resulting from the first experiment for rule 56 medically sound to make the diagnosis? The suggested experiments can lead the expert into reconsidering the lists of major and minor findings for a particular final diagnosis and to possibly change these findings.

> If rule 56 had been satisfied, 8 currently misdiagnosed MCTD cases
> would have been diagnosed correctly. Currently, rule 56 is not used
> incorrectly in any of the cases with diagnoses other than MCTD. In
> rule 56 the component missing with the greatest frequency is "Major".
>
> Therefore, we suggest to Decrease the number of majors in rule 56.
> This would generalize the rule so that it will be easier to satisfy.

Figure 1-15: Example of Support for an Experiment

One is not absolutely certain of a net gain in performance before an experiment is tried. In the case of a generalization experiment, there may be more than one unsatisfied component in a rule marked for generalization; the marking procedure picks the *first* unsatisfied component in the rule.

1.14 Modifying the Model

After an experiment to revise the rules has been determined, the model designer can test his proposed revision on the cases. This is facilitated by editing capabilities which permit the model designer to interrogate and to modify the rules in the model. The changes are logged separately from the rules in the model so that the original rules can be restored. The editing functions include changing:

- the number of major or minor observations,

- the requirement component,

- the exclusion component,

- any rule reaching an intermediate result which is used by other rules.

Continuing with our example, Figure 1-16 shows SEEK's response to the model designer's suggested change of rule 56. It recommends changing the number of major required by rule 56 to be 2. The commands that allow the model designer to interrogate and to modify the rules require rule numbers or symbolic labels to reference parts of the model.

Rule   56 is:

3 or more Majors for MCTD
→ Possible Mixed connective tissue disease

Generalization   of Rule   56 is:

2 or more Majors for MCTD
→ Possible Mixed connective tissue disease

Figure 1-16:   Example of Rule Modification

1.15 Reviewing the Impact of the Refinement Experiments

The results of a specific experiment are obtained by conditionally incorporating the revised rule(s) into the model. The updated model is then executed on the data base of cases. The results are summarized in Figure 1-17 for making the change to rule 56. In this example, such a modification significantly improves performance. Several misdiagnosed mixed connective tissue disease cases are now correctly diagnosed by the model. Moreover, there was no adverse side effect of this change on other cases with different stored conclusions. The model designer has the option either to accept or to reject the experiment. If a simple modification does not lead to desirable results, more complicated changes may be tried, such as multiple modifications or dropping a condition in a requirement.

	Before		False Positives	After		False Positives
MCTD	9/ 33	(27%)	0	17/ 33	(52%)	0
Others	80/ 88	(91%)		80/ 88	(91%)	
Total	89/121	(74%)		97/121	(80%)	
Others						
RA	42/ 42	(100%)	9	42/ 42	(100%)	8
SLE	12/ 18	(67%)	4	12/ 18	(67%)	3
PSS	22/ 23	(96%)	5	22/ 23	(96%)	3
PM	4/ 5	(80%)	1	4/ 5	(80%)	1

Figure 1-17:   Summary of Before/After Performance

1.16 Discussion

The tabular model appears to be a reasonable framework for encoding expert knowledge in a real and complex application. Excellent performance was achieved for the diagnosis of connective tissue disease [24]. This approach has proven particularly valuable in assisting the expert in domains where two diagnoses are difficult to distinguish. For example, there are no definitive clinical criteria to confirm the diagnoses in the connective tissue disease area. The experts obtain by means of empirical testing a measure of the usefulness of the observations expressed in the tabular model.

There are limitations to this approach--for some applications it may be difficult to express rules using major and minor observations or using only 3 levels of confidence. Although this model may not be the most expressive model for capturing expert knowledge, it is a model which is suitable for an empirical analysis leading to experimentation with rule refinement. Most samples of cases are not completely representative and cannot begin to match the scope of an expert's knowledge. But as others have found [14] even with small samples of cases, empirical evidence can be of great value in designing and verifying an expert model.

Ideally, a tabular model abstracts the expert's reasoning while the cases provide evidence that the model is accurate. SEEK attempts to achieve this harmony by pointing out potential problems with these dual sources of knowledge. Given the performance of the cases, potential problems with the rules can be identified with the tools described earlier. The summarized performance results are a means for the expert to rethink a tabular model that is performing poorly for a specific diagnosis. The analysis of the tabular rules based on case experience sharply focuses the expert's attention on modifications that potentially result in improved performance and are also medically sound. This can lead to reviewing individual cases for inaccuracies in the data and to reconsidering the importance of specific criteria in the model. This process is not intended to custom-craft rules solely to the cases, but rather to provide the expert with explicit performance information that should prove helpful for interactive modification of the rules.

In developing expert systems, we recognize that an expert's knowledge cannot be directly learned from sample cases except in highly limited situations. In the past, case review has been used solely to verify the performance of an expert model. If, however, we begin with both a set of expert modeled rules and representative sample cases, we have the basis for a more valuable interactive tool for rule refinement. With systems that integrate performance analysis into a model design framework, the expert will obtain a better formulation of the model and a better understanding of the explicit diagnostic criteria that he uses in his reasoning [32].

2. Background

In this chapter, we review research on knowledge acquisition from the perspective of building expert consultation programs. Specifically, we are concerned about methods for building a rule-based consultation program for classification-type problems. For a medical diagnosis application, such a program may be described as containing:

1. a set of diagnostic conclusions that stand for the program's possible answers,

2. a set of findings (i.e., observations or features) that stand for the program's questions and are relevant in reaching the conclusions,

3. a set of rules that relate the findings with the conclusions.

The operation of a program using a knowledge base of this kind first gathers some data about a patient. The questioning strategy can be as simple as reading a patient record from a data base file with little else required of the user, or it may be guided by the program's reasoning component to ask questions that are related to previous responses. In either case, once enough data is gathered a control strategy directs the consultation for the classification task and decides which conclusions best match the case data. Building such a program usually starts with a specification of the diagnostic conclusions and the findings, and knowledge acquisition consists of formulating the rules that relate the findings to the conclusions. With this basic description of the classification program in mind, section 2.1 reviews case-derived methods of knowledge acquisition and section 2.2 surveys expert-derived techniques in expert system development and evaluation.

2.1 Case-derived Methods

Reviewed below are techniques that use sample cases alone to derive decision-making rules. Using a set of cases alone can be especially difficult for realistic and large-scale medical diagnostic applications where the dimensionality is large both in the numbers of findings and conclusions and there is much uncertainty in the diagnostic reasoning. In these applications, a set of cases rarely covers the range of possible ways of arriving at diagnostic conclusions which an expert physician has experienced. The expert physician can specify domain-specific information in expert modeled rules that is lacking in the cases and cover many more situations than in a set of cases.

2.1.1 Statistical and Pattern Recognition Approaches

The formulation of various classifiers as mathematical discriminant functions have used statistical decision theory methods [13], [8]; and [19] presented one of the early decriptions of these methods for medical applications. When sufficient statistics are available, one can obtain very good performance by discriminant functions that have been formulated using Bayes' rule [44]. Although Bayesian methods can achieve optimal classification that satisfies minimum average risk or error-rate criteria, problems of dimensionality and mutual exclusivity of conclusions are important limitations in the application of these methods. These and other shortcomings of the Bayesian methods are discussed in [41]. If reasonable statistics are available (i.e., from a data base of patient records such as ARAMIS [11], [12]) and even if conditional independence is relaxed, a large set of observations impose computational demands to obtain for combinations of observations the conditional and prior probabilities required of these methods. Early pattern recognition techniques [29] used the samples of cases directly to build classifiers of discriminant functions. Here, the basic process is one of adjusting weights of features in a linear discriminant function in response to the current classification assigned to a training sample. For a subclass of problems, it is known that this adjustment process converges if the training samples are linearly separable, or that the probability distributions of the features are nonoverlapping. Another pattern recognition method--the *nearest neighbor* technique--is based on the acquisition of a few prototypical samples, which are then used to classify new samples based on various closeness measures.

In general, statistical pattern recognition methods work well for limited-sized applications. Better methods are needed to reduce the dimensionality for realistic large-scale problem areas. When the discriminators are put to use they are generally "black-box" systems [18]. That is, the interaction is limited to entering data, from which the conclusions are derived in a mathematical way that is not readily understandable by the expert. Because of this difficulty of explaining in familiar terms how the classifier used the data in reaching its results, it is generally recognized that these methods are unacceptable in applications such as medical consultation tasks where human confidence in the results is essential [17], [36].

34

2.1.2 Artificial Intelligence Approaches

A central concern in the design of AI learning programs is the internal representation for the rule to be learned. Many AI learning schemes have appeared in the literature over the past two decades (e.g., [35], [45], [25], [52], [5], [48],) and comparative reviews of learning systems and methods have appeared in [37], [7], and [27]. While much work has been done, very few have reached the point of being used in a real application [5], and experimentation has usually been in problem areas with relatively small dimensions and noise-free data.

In this section, we review two learning schemes in relation to SEEK. SEEK's method for the analysis of the cases focuses on a subset of rules by gathering empirical information suggesting the generalization and specialization of rules in the set. This can be viewed as a learning system which limits changes to refinements of existing rules.

The terms generalization and specialization are used in the version space approach [26]. Here, two sets of rules are maintained as bounds on the *maximally specialized* rules and the *maximally generalized* rules that are consistent with the training cases presented for a conclusion, where the range of expressions is based on a partial ordering of objects in the domain. A training case is prespecified as either *positive* - a rule must be found to cover the case, or *negative* - no rule should match the case. The scheme seeks to cover all positive cases while allowing no negative cases to match any of the rules. There are no certainty values assigned to the rules in the version space. The version space method converges on a rule set provided that the cases are noise-free and accurately diagnosed, and that the language underlying the partial ordering is sufficiently expressive to accurately describe the training cases. An important result of this work is that the condition under which the language for the partial ordering may need revision occurs when the version space collapses. In contrast, the scheme implemented in SEEK refines expert-derived rules that have been categorized by confidence levels in the model. Correct classification for all cases is not required. That is, a negative case is allowed to be covered so long as there is a rule for another conclusion which overrides the matched rule(s). A rule is marked for generalization or specialization based on the comparison of the certainty values assigned to the conclusion of the expert and the conclusion reached by the model. Finally, our scheme is interactive in nature requiring the involvement of the model designer. It is not intended to be an autonomous learning system.

The EURISKO program [21] [22] is related to SEEK in that the analysis of previous problem-solving experience forms the basis for finding an improved formulation of the rules. EURISKO abstracts or revises rules used in the task of searching for concepts and relationships in a domain.

In EURISKO, rules and meta-rules for abstracting or revising the rules, are represented by frames and organized into a hierarchy of frames. This is different than the representation of the rules in AM [20] where the rules were associated with particular slots in domain concept frames. The idea of putting the rules into frames is that it facilitates their change by using the same control strategy applied to the domain concepts. In one application, naval fleet design, the abstraction/revision process is based on an analysis of several simulated battles with particular naval fleet configurations. He [21] reports that for the naval fleet design task, a 60/40% breakdown in the attribution to the human vs. EURISKO for abstracting relevant rules. This is one of several problems in which EURISKO has been successfully applied, yet it is difficult to know how the automatic abstraction/revision occurs, i.e., the assignment of credit and blame to rules, and how this information is put to use in the process of changing the rules.

In the SEEK scheme, we have used a fixed-means of assigning a rule's credit or blame from the deterministic scoring function applied to each tabular model. In case analysis, predictive information is derived and made available to SEEK's heuristic rules in the form of summarized statistics for the purpose of suggesting rule refinements.

2.2 Expert System Evaluation and Development

In this section, we review techniques for the evaluation and development of expert systems.

2.2.1 Evaluation

Various representational schemes and decision-making strategies have been applied for expert system development. However, there have been few published results concerning the evaluation of expert systems. The evaluations of CASNET [23], MYCIN [53], and PROSPECTOR [14] [15] have shown the systems to perform at a comparable level of performance with experts in glaucoma, infectious diseases, and geologic mineral deposit analysis, respectively.

The key point about these studies is that evaluation occurred at the end of the development cycle of the respective knowledge bases. The CASNET, PROSPECTOR, and MYCIN studies each reported performance results on a few cases. Intermediate as well as final conclusions reached by the consultation program were evaluated for each case. In contrast, our work in the development of a rheumatology model (section 1.6 reviews this project) has concentrated on the analysis of a large set of cases. Because the scoring function of a model is a direct assignment of weight from rules to conclusions, evaluation of intermediate results can be directly traced from final conclusions. Evaluation and analysis in SEEK are based on a comparison of the expert's final conclusion with the model's final conclusion.

As a result of PROSPECTOR's evaluation, the process was deemed to be a worthwhile part of the development cycle. Case review served a useful purpose in revising the model, and it was concluded that it should be integrated into the model development process.

In PROSPECTOR, production rules are used for representing judgmental knowledge and semantic networks represent descriptive knowledge about the domain. Reasoning is primarily based on subjective bayesian methods which assign and propagate weights to hypotheses. PROSPECTOR's knowledge acquisition and editing program (KAS [34]) assists the model designer in building and modifying the networks. One of its valuable functions is to show the effect of the propagation of weight changes on hypotheses during a consultation session on a case. Because of the many uncertainty measures usually associated with the geologic domain models in PROSPECTOR, sensitivity analysis techniques have been developed to test the model's stability. However, knowledge acquisition and evaluation is carried out on only a small number of cases.

Another system that aided case review is the TEIRESIAS program [6], initially developed as a knowledge acquisition assistant for MYCIN [36]. TEIRESIAS acquires knowledge directly from the human expert and gives him the capability of seeing his rules applied on a case. Within the context of a consultation session, this method interactively guides the expert through the knowledge base of rules and has been shown to help the expert find errors with his rules and correct them directly for the consultation at hand. The primary kind of assistance is in the acquisition of new rules to correct erroneous conclusions reached in the consultation. In this case, a rule model (meta rule) which contains a summarization of information about a rule's form and likely content is used to check against a new rule proposed by the expert. The rule model is automatically generated from the existing set of rules in the knowledge base.

In TEIRESIAS, the process of interacting with the user follows the rules according to MYCIN's goal-directed control strategy. Briefly, an AND/OR goal tree of clauses (conclusions and premise clauses in rules) is constructed as a result of invoking rules in the backward direction. To determine if a goal is satisfied (e.g., whether to conclude a disease) all applicable rules for the goal are invoked. After all of these rules are evaluated and assigned weights, the original goal is evaluated by applying a scoring function on all rule weights contributing to the goal.

Traversal of this goal tree by TEIRESIAS facilitates the expert's understanding of the consultation and reduces the burden of isolating rules, especially when several rules contribute to reaching a conclusion. When changes are made to the knowledge base to correct an erroneous conclusion in a consultation, there is no direct check of these changes on other cases previously processed by the consultation program.

2.2.2 Generalized Knowledge Engineering Tools

There has been much work in providing general frameworks for developing expert systems, such as AGE [28], OPS [9], HEARSAY III [3], EXPERT [49], and EMYCIN [42]. The latter two have been built specifically to facilitate the construction and testing of classification-type expert systems. EXPERT and EMYCIN provide the expert system builder with a prespecified control strategy, a production rule formalism for encoding expert knowledge, explanatory tools for tracing the execution of rules during a consultation session, and a data base system in which cases can be stored for empirical testing. We have based SEEK on EXPERT, and will now review some of its key features.

EXPERT is a system designed to facilitate the construction and testing of expert consultation models. Several representational formats for using production rules are available. Knowledge is compiled in EXPERT, offering efficiency in processing individual cases. Unlike most other expert system design frameworks, a distinction is made in the EXPERT formalism between hypotheses and findings, following the traditional characterization of classification problems. The representational formalisms and control strategy have been chosen to make model design a simple and easy process (especially for those unfamiliar with computers.) Model design follows a few fixed requirements in the organization of an EXPERT model. A model consists of three sections. The *Hypotheses* section describes the conclusions to be reached by the model, which they can be organized according to final diagnostic, final treatment, and intermediate conclusions. The *Findings* section describes the questions to be asked of the user in the consultation session. The *Rules* section describes rules for:

1. controlling the questioning of the session,

2. logically relating findings directly to conclusions,

3. logically relating findings and (intermediate) conclusions to other conclusions.

An example of the EXPERT model structure appears in Appendix II. Confidence values are assigned to conclusions within the numeric range of -1 and 1 [49], where -1 indicates complete denial, and 1 complete confirmation. An event-driven control strategy is employed. The scoring function has been deliberately made modular where parts can be turned on or off to accommodate various reasoning strategies depending on the model designer's preference for the application at hand. The scoring function is based on a direct assignment of the largest absolute weight among competing rules of findings-to-hypotheses, offering the model designer predictability in evaluating a model's results. Additional weights can be included from taxonomies and other rules.

A data base system maintains cases for which logical queries can be made to retrieve statistical information on groups of cases. An important component of the EXPERT design system is an automatic case conversion module. It is used to assess the effect of a modification to the model on all cases in the data base. Significant changes in the weights of all conclusions in all cases are noted by the case conversion module.

In EMYCIN, a LISP-based production rule formalism is used for expressing inferential knowledge, and a goal-directed control strategy is employed. An Algol-like language is used to ease the model designer's expression of rules. The facilities for evaluating the knowledge base of an EMYCIN consultation program include an explanation capability to trace through the goal-tree of rules during and after a consultation session. Changes to the knowledge base can be checked by running previously correct cases in batch mode, where the user must specify relevant intermediate and final conclusions for evaluation purposes to the batch processor.

2.3 Summary

The expert system design frameworks have provided reasonable representations to encode expert knowledge from various domains; EXPERT and EMYCIN have been applied to several medical and non-medical application areas. In some areas [4] [50], scoring functions that combine rule weights have not been needed. However, problems remain in determining how to best use scoring functions in handling approximate reasoning. This has been particularly important in medical applications, and better methods are needed to understand a model's behavior.

The KAS and TEIRESIAS programs provide great assistance in reducing the burden of the expert in unraveling and understanding the effect of the scoring function, but this is done after a knowledge base is substantially developed and on a case-by-case basis. Schemes such as EXPERT give the model designer the choice of specifying the amount of weighting to be incorporated in the reasoning process. For medical applications this is important, in helping elicit decision-making knowledge from the domain expert where he will ideallly be able to write his rules with a solid understanding of how they are going to be used by the program.

Past experience with knowledge acquisition and evaluation methods in expert systems can be summarized as follows:

1. automatic learning from samples of cases have been applied to areas with relatively small dimensions, adequate statistics, or having relatively noise-free and accurate case data;

2. revising or abstracting rules based on an analysis of previous problem solving experience requires an effective means to credit and blame rules;

3. evaluation techniques have been applied after a system's knowledge base has been developed and primarily on a case-by-case basis;

4. while expert system developments have produced adequate representations, difficulties in understanding a model's behavior have persisted; and adjustment of scoring functions have been left to the designer, with assistance of knowledge-base editing programs.

In SEEK, the cases are used for testing an expert-derived model. Although cases may have errors in their data, the use of SEEK assumes that the correct diagnosis stored with each case is accurately presented. A scoring function that assigns weight from a single rule is uniformly applied to each diagnosis in the tabular model. This facilitates a direct assignment of credit and blame to the rules for predicting rule modifications. Finally, empirical testing is integrated into the design stage of a model. SEEK uses performance results over all cases to propose experiments about rule refinement for improving a model's performance. Experiments are tested directly for empirical verification of the content of the knowledge base.

3. Methods for Gathering Rule Refinement Statistics

3.1 Introduction

Information must be gathered to recognize and assess the positive or negative aspects in a rule's past performance, so that refinements that will improve the model's performance can be found. For instance, the TEREISIAS system [6] assists the expert in correcting a single misdiagnosed case by providing a guided trace of the execution of the rules. An explanation about an erroneous conclusion reached by the model is derived from the rules cited in the trace. With this in mind, the goal of this chapter is to show how case analysis methods are applied on the rules in a tabular model and for each misdiagnosed case in a data base of test cases. These methods cite rules as reasons for incorrect conclusions and use these reasons to suggest rule refinements. This chapter provides the basis for describing heuristic rules that suggest experiments about rule refinement. Methods of case analysis are described to gather performance statistics about a model's rules in order to evaluate the heuristic rules. The heuristics are described in chapter 4.

As noted earlier, analysis of a case is based on comparing the model's confidence in both the expert's conclusion and the model's conclusion. A case is misdiagnosed by the model if the expert's conclusion does not match the model's conclusion. The expert's conclusion is stored with the case, while the model's conclusion is taken as that conclusion reached with the greatest certainty. Implicit in the analysis of a misdiagnosed case is the ability to answer two questions about the performance of the model:

- why wasn't the expert's conclusion reached with greatest certainty?

- why was the model's conclusion reached?

Knowledge that is needed to answer these questions is readily obtained because a model's confidence in each conclusion can be directly determined from the single rule that was satisfied with the greatest certainty.

This chapter is divided into three main sections. Sections 3.2 and 3.3 describe case analysis methods which are applied to the rules in cases misdiagnosed by the model. Section 3.2 describes the method of case analysis to generalize rules for the expert's conclusion. Section 3.3 describes the method of analysis to specialize rules for the model's incorrect conclusion. Section 3.4 summarizes the statistics that are gathered by these case analysis methods.

3.2 Generalization: Rule Analysis for the Expert's Conclusion

For each misdiagnosed case, a trace is performed on the rules applicable in reaching the expert's conclusion. We want to correct a misdiagnosed case by changing rules for the expert's conclusion. Several rules are usually applicable for generalization and each can be weakened in many ways. For instance, a condition in a rule can be removed; numeric threshold values for the numbers of majors or minors can be decreased; and a rule's confidence level can be increased without changing the rule's conditions. These specific kinds of rule changes are similar to other generalization methods that appear in the literature; for comparative review of generalization methods, [7] have characterized various kinds of generalization such as a *Dropping Condition Rule*.

We begin by looking for rules for the expert's conclusion which would correct the misdiagnosed case by simply increasing their assigned confidence levels. In order to do this, we identify satisfied rules pointing to the expert's conclusion which were overridden by rules for other conclusions.

As an alternative to increasing a rule's confidence we could try changing the conditions in a rule. In order to do this, we look for *partially satisfied* rules which require as little modification as possible in order to be satisfied. Next, we must separate the partially satisfied rules which would correct the case from those which would not. To select a candidate rule for generalization, we analyze the subset of partially satisfied rules which would correct the case. In summary, there are four steps in the trace:

1. **identify satisfied rules for the expert's conclusion**

2. **find partially satisfied rules**

3. **find possible rules to generalize**

4. **select a candidate rule to generalize**

In Figure 3-1, we show a trace of a misdiagnosed case. The summary of the model's performance on case 14 includes a statement of the expert's conclusion of mixed connective tissue disease. Rule 89 with an assigned confidence of *possible* is satisfied for mixed connective tissue disease. Rule 66 is responsible for reaching the model's incorrect

44

CASE: 14

Expert conclusion: Mixed connective tissue disease
Model   conclusion: Probable Rheumatoid arthritis

This is the rule for the expert's conclusion:

Rule 89:   2 or more Majors for MCTD (MJMCT) (2 Majors Satisfied)
            Requirement 1 for Possible MCTD (RS102) (Satisfied)
            --> Possible Mixed connective tissue disease   (MCTD)

This is the rule for the model's conclusion:

Rule 66:   2 or more Majors for RA (MJRA) (2 Majors Satisfied)
            2 or more Minors for RA (MNRA) (2 Minors Satisfied)
            No Exclusion 1 for Probable RA (ER101) (Satisfied)
            --> Probable Rheumatoid arthritis   (RA)

Figure 3-1:   Example of a Misdiagnosed Case

conclusion of probable rheumatoid arthritis.   The first step in the trace is to determine whether there are any satisfied rules for the expert's conclusion in the case.   This is equivalent to checking if the expert's conclusion was reached by the model with a confidence greater than zero.   This is done to identify rules that could be modified by changing the confidence for the satisfied rule from its current level to some higher level (e.g., changing the rule's confidence from possible to probable.)   In case 14, rule 89 is the single satisfied rule for mixed connective tissue disease.   If there are no satisfied rules, then all rules are traced looking for partially satisfied rules that consist of one or more satisfied components (e.g., one or more Major findings, or a satisfied requirement).   For case 14, we traced the unsatisfied rules which directly conclude mixed connective tissue disease, of which there are 6 in the model.   These rules are shown in Figure 3-2, referenced by their internal rule numbers (88 through 93).

Rule 88:   1 or more Majors for MCTD (MJMCT) (2 Majors Satisfied)
3 or more Minors for MCTD   (MNMCT) (1 Minors Satisfied)
Requirement 1 for Possible MCTD   (RS102) (Satisfied)
--> Possible Mixed connective tissue disease   (MCTD)

Rule 89:   2 or more Majors for MCTD   (MJMCT) (2 Majors Satisfied)
Requirement 1 for Possible MCTD   (RS102) (Satisfied)
--> Possible Mixed connective tissue disease   (MCTD)

Rule 90:   3 or more Majors for MCTD   (MJMCT) (2 Majors Satisfied)
--> Possible Mixed connective tissue disease   (MCTD)

Rule 91:   2 or more Majors for MCTD   (MJMCT) (2 Majors Satisfied)
2 or more Minors for MCTD   (MNMCT) (1 Minors Satisfied)
Requirement 1 for Probable MCTD   (RR102) (Not Satisfied)
--> Probable Mixed connective tissue disease   (MCTD)

Rule 92:   3 or more Majors for MCTD   (MJMCT) (2 Majors Satisfied)
Requirement 2 for Probable MCTD   (RR202) (Not Satisfied)
--> Probable Mixed connective tissue disease   (MCTD)

Rule 93:   4 or more Majors for MCTD   (MJMCT) (2 Majors Satisfied)
Requirement 1 for Definite MCTD   (RD102) (Not Satisfied)
No Exclusion 1 for Definite MCTD   (ED102) (Not Satisfied)
--> Definite Mixed connective tissue disease   (MCTD)

Figure 3-2:   Rules for Mixed Connective Tissue Disease

3.2.1 Determining Partially Satisfied Rules

To put the next two sections into perspective, our goal is to correct a misdiagnosed case by refining the rules for the expert's conclusion. We want to select a candidate rule for generalization which currently is unsatisfied but, if it were satisfied, would correct the case. This implies that the kind of refinement we're seeking is the removal of specific components in the candidate rule. The purpose of these two sections is to describe the steps which lead to the selection of a candidate rule for generalization. Finally, we state that the selection of a candidate rule for generalization is a suggestion in correcting a misdiagnosed case and is recorded as a statistic to support the refinement of this rule. The statistic is gathered for each misdiagnosed case according to the methods described below.

Next we describe a method for tracing the rules for the expert's conclusion in a misdiagnosed case. As a result of a consultation session on a case, a rule can be found to be satisfied (and its conclusion infered by the model), or a rule can be found to be unsatisfied. Given a misdiagnosed case, our method of analysis is focused on the unsatisfied rules for the expert's conclusion because we want to identify rules which may need to be *weakened* in order to correct the case. In our example of case 14, we want to refine the rules for the conclusion of mixed connective tissue disease. Among the unsatisfied rules for the expert's conclusion, we're particularly interested in *partially satisfied rules*. A partially satisfied rule is one which consists of at least one component satisfied by the case data, while also containing at least one component that is unsatisfied by the case data. Partially satisfied rules provide empirical evidence that is summarized by a measure reflecting a rule's percentage of total satisfaction. The measure is used to determine candidate rules for generalization, and the tracing procedure described below is used to derive it.

Each of the unsatisfied rules for the expert's conclusion is traced to determine the rule's percentage of total satisfaction by the case data. This is done by maintaining two counts:

- **the number of satisfied components;**

- **the number of components needed for satisfaction.**

Before describing this counting procedure, we must specify the structure of the rules that it is applied to. Each rule in the model consists of a conjunction of one or more components, where a component is identified as one of the following types:

- **Finding** - the component expresses either an observation which is asked directly of the user during the questioning stage of a consultation session, or it expresses numbers of majors or numbers of minors;

- **Intermediate** - the component expresses a conclusion that has rules concluding it;

- **Disjunction** - the component expresses a list of findings or intermediate components, a certain number of which is needed for satisfaction.

An example of a rule containing these types of components is shown in Figure 3-3. At the top level, rule 88 consists of a conjunction of three components which are taken from the tabular model format of numbers of majors, minors, and a requirement. These components are detailed in the graphical representation of the rule, where its hierarchical organization in a tabular model is illustrated. Note that the requirement component labeled RS102 is expanded in the tree to illustrate the specific components which were used in reaching RS102.

The components of type *finding* are labeled: 1 major, 3 minors, RNP, ENANP, and ENANH. There is one component of type *intermediate*, labeled RS102; and the component labeled ENAM is a *disjunction*.

Rule 88:   1 or more Majors for MCTD   (MJMCT) (2 Majors Satisfied)
            3 or more Minors for MCTD   (MNMCT) (1 Minors Satisfied)
            Requirement 1 for Possible MCTD   (RS102) (Satisfied)
            --> Possible Mixed connective tissue disease   (MCTD)

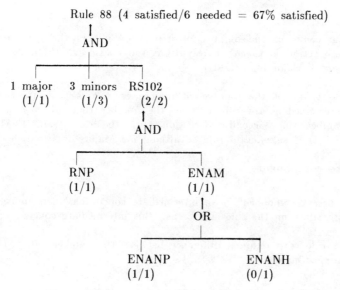

Figure 3-3:   Trace of a Partially Satisfied Rule

The counting procedure is organized into 3 steps according to the type of component encountered in a rule. A discussion of each step including an example for each one follows the procedure. For each rule, the procedure scans the rule left to right and examines each component according to these steps:

1. Finding component

    a. If the current component expresses a single finding value:

        i. the count of the number *needed* for satisfaction is one;

        ii. the count of the number *satisfied* is one if the finding value is satisfied in the case, and zero otherwise.

    b. If the current component expresses numbers of majors or numbers of minors:

        i. the count of the number of majors or minors that are *needed* for satisfaction is taken directly from the clause (e.g. rule 88 *needs* at least 1 Major for MCTD);

        ii. the count of the number of majors or minors that are *satisfied* is determined as the minimum of the number that are *needed* and the number that actually were found in the case (e.g., 1 Major for MCTD is *satisfied* in rule 88 although 2 Majors appeared in case 14).

2. Intermediate component

    a. If the current component is an intermediate conclusion, then apply the rule trace procedure on the rules that reach this intermediate conclusion;

    b. Select a rule with minimal difference between the number *satisfied* and the number *needed.*

        i. increment the count of the number *needed* for rule satisfaction by the result obtained from tracing the rules for the intermediate conclusion;

        ii. increment the count of the number *satisfied* for this rule by the result obtained from tracing the rules for the intermediate conclusion.

3. Disjunctive component

    a. If the current component expresses a disjunction of K components that are *needed* for satisfaction from N choices (e.g., 2 components of these 3 choices are needed: a, b, or c), then apply the rule trace procedure on each of the N choices; the results are N separate pairs of values *needed/satisfied.*

    b. Select the K maximally satisfied components and sum up the respective *needed* and *satisfied* values;

        i. increment the count of the number *needed* for the rule containing the disjunction by the result obtained above for tracing the components in the N choice, K needed disjunction;

ii. increment the count of the number *satisfied* for the rule containing the disjunction by the result obtained above for tracing the clauses in the **N** choice, **K** needed disjunction.

The three steps in this counting procedure can be explained as follows. A component of type *finding* usually is asked of the user during a consultation session. It represents the most primitive piece of information about the case data in a model. A finding is an observation, which in the medical domains typically refers to items such as "fever greater than 38 degrees C" or a laboratory result such as "positive antibody to RNP". A valid response for a finding is *yes, no, unknown,* or a *numerical* result. Whether a response for a finding is pertinent in reaching a conclusion is determined by its use in the rules. To determine a finding's satisfaction in a rule, a truth value is associated with the finding in the rule. If the response to a finding satisfies the truth value condition specified in a rule, then the finding is satisfied; otherwise it is unsatisfied. Because of this simple two-state outcome, the finding value in the step **(1a.)** is either one or zero. In our example in Figure 3-3, the value for the number *needed* for satisfaction by each of the findings RNP, ENANP and ENANH is one, while the value for the number *satisfied* is taken from the case data as 1, 1, and 0, respectively. In a similar way, we treat each major or minor *satisfied* as a finding and the sum of these values is compared with the number of majors or minors *needed* for satisfaction by the rule. This follows from step **(1b.)**.

The *intermediate* component is labeled RS102 in our example in Figure 3-3. By definition this component has rules which conclude it, and therefore, these rules must be traced to obtain a percentage of total satisfaction for the component. A rule which concludes RS102 and which is selected in step **(2b.)** is shown in the figure. According to step **(2b.)**, this rule has a minimal difference between the number *needed* and the number *satisfied*. This rule is satisfied by the data since the finding RNP is satisfied and the *disjunctive* component labeled ENAM is satisfied. How the disjunction is scored is determined by step **(3.)**. Only one component of 2 is *needed* to satisfy ENAM. In summary, the trace of a rule is governed by the 3 types of components which can appear in a rule. Depending on the type of component encountered, either finding, intermediate, or disjunctive, a distinct scoring scheme is applied. The results are summed to arrive at a measure about the rule's percentage of satisfaction. This measure is used to determine a candidate rule to generalize by selecting a rule with maximum percentage of satisfaction.

3.2.2 Finding Rules to Generalize

The result of the rule trace procedure is a percentage of total satisfaction for each rule. Figure 3-3 illustrates the trace procedure for one of the rules (rule 88) that concludes mixed connective tissue disease. In Figure 3-3, the components labeled: 1 major, 3 minors, RNP, ENANP, and ENANH are identified as type *finding*; the component labeled RS102 is an *intermediate* component; and, the component labeled ENAM is a *disjunction*. Thus, in this case, the percentage of satisfaction for rule 88 is 67%.

A summary of the trace of partially satisfied rules is shown below in Figure 3-4 where the rules for mixed connective tissue disease are organized by confidence level. Five of the 6 rules for mixed connective tissue disease are partially satisfied in case 14. For each partially satisfied rule found, its confidence is compared with the confidence assigned to the model's conclusion. If the confidence for a partially satisfied rule overrides that for the model's conclusion, the partially satisfied rule is added to a list of *possible rules to generalize*. This list indicates that each of the rules would correct the case if it were satisfied. We want to select one of the rules as a candidate for generalization. Rules 91 92 and 93 are added to the list of *possible rules to generalize*, because each of these partially satisfied rules would correct case 14 if it were satisfied. (Recall we had assumed that ties in confidence between the expert's conclusion and the model's different conclusion are acceptable. Therefore, rules 91 and 92 with an assigned confidence of probable would override the model's incorrect conclusion of probable rheumatoid arthritis in case 14.)

Confidence	Definite	Probable		Possible		
Rule number	93	92	91	90	89	88
Percentage of rule satisfied	57%	60%	71%	67%	100%	67%

Figure 3-4:   Performance of a Subset of Rules on a Case

3.2.3 Selecting a Candidate Rule to Generalize

The previous two sections described how a measure about rule performance is obtained from a trace of each of the partially satisfied rules for the expert's conclusion. This is part of the case analysis process which is intended to derive a suggestion in the form of a statistic about the generalization of a rule. This section can be viewed as the concluding step in the case analysis. We want to select a candidate rule to generalize based on the performance of the partially satisfied rules.

52

A heuristic procedure shown in Figure 3-5 is applied to the list of possible generalizable rules in order to be actually generalized.

1. the rule concludes at a confidence level which least exceeds that for the model's incorrect conclusion;

2. the rule contains the maximum number of satisfied components for all rules concluding at that level.

Figure 3-5: Closeness Measure for Selecting a Rule to Generalize

Rule 91 is selected in case 14 because it concludes at a minimum confidence level probable) needed to correct the case while being the most satisfied rule (71% satisfied, rom Figure 3-4) among all rules concluding at that confidence level. Finally, the rule is lisplayed with information supporting its generalization. This information includes the dentification number of the case, the model's incorrect conclusion, and the first unsatisfied omponent found in the candidate rule. This is shown in Figure 3-6 for case 14.

> There exists 1 partially satisfied rule for MCTD with weight
> assignment >= than that set by RA rule

> Rule 91: 2 or more Majors for MCTD (MJMCT) (2 Majors Satisfied)
> 2 or more Minors for MCTD (MNMCT) (1 Minors Satisfied)
> Requirement 1 for Probable MCTD (RR102) (Not Satisfied)
> --> Probable Mixed connective tissue disease (MCTD)

Information supporting generalization of rule 91:

Case	Model's conclusion	Unsatisfied component in rule 91
14	RA	MNMCT

Figure 3-6: Generalization of Rule 91 for Case 14

Rule 91 is a partially satisfied rule for the expert's conclusion which, if satisfied, will verride the incorrect diagnosis of rheumatoid arthritis reached by rule 66 in case 14. urther, the minors component in rule 91 is the first unsatisfied component found that is entified to be weakened. Note that the requirement component in rule 91 also is nsatisfied for case 14. In this case, weakening the minors component (e.g. dropping the umber of minors required to "1 or more minors for MCTD") is a *necessary*, although not sufficient modification of rule 91 to correct case 14.

3.2.4 Summary: Rule Analysis for the Expert's Conclusion

We started with a misdiagnosed case and knowledge about why the expert's conclusion was not reached with greatest certainty. A tracing procedure is applied to the rules for the expert's conclusion in order to identify a candidate rule to generalize. The strongest satisfied rule for the expert's conclusion is identified so that its assigned confidence might be increased to override the model's incorrect conclusion. The rules that were not satisfied in the case with confidence exceeding that for the model's incorrect conclusion are searched, looking for partially satisfied rules, which are then added to a list of *possible rules to generalize*. After tracing the rules, a heuristic procedure finds a candidate rule for generalization by selecting one partially satisfied rule from those on the list of *possible rules to generalize*, such that it is the *closest* to being satisfied. As a result, a candidate rule for generalization is identified by marking it with information supporting its generalization. In summary, the answers to two subquestions were sought:

1. Were there any satisfied rules for the expert's conclusion? If there were, then the misdiagnosed case might be corrected by increasing the confidence levels on these satisfied rules.[1]

2. Were there any partially satisfied rules that would correctly diagnose the case if they were satisfied? If there were, then the misdiagnosed case might be corrected by removing unsatisfied components from the left-hand side of these rules.

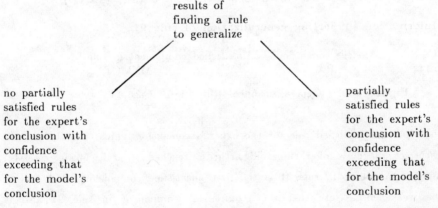

Figure 3-7:   Determining a Rule to Generalize for the Expert's Conclusion

---

[1]While this is a simple change, it is a potentially drastic one for the expert. The point is that the expert writes his rules with specific levels of confidence in mind. Because of this, changing a rule's confidence would mean that the whole rule is in error and not just a specific component in the rule. Even if a rule is *moved* from one confidence level to another, the expert's belief in the importance of criteria in the rule is changed relative to other rules. This is discussed more fully in Chapter 4 on specifying the conditions to suggest changing a rule's confidence.

3.2.5 Discussion

Rule analysis for the expert's conclusion does not guarantee that a candidate rule for generalization will be found for every misdiagnosed case. There may be no rules available for the expert's conclusion that could otherwise override the model's incorrect conclusion. Alternatively, there may be rules available for the expert's conclusion in the model, but no partially satisfied rules that would correct a case if they were satisfied. In the situation where ties in confidence between the expert's conclusion and the model's different conclusion have been predetermined to be incorrect, there could never be a guarantee of finding a candidate rule for generalization in every misdiagnosed case. This is easily seen by considering a case in which the model's incorrect conclusion is reached at the definite confidence level. Using the tabular model, with its organization based on the three confidence levels, it will be impossible to find a rule to possibly generalize in this case. On the other hand, the chances that a candidate rule for generalization would be found in each misdiagnosed case might be improved when ties are predetermined to be correct. But the problem in this situation arises when no partially satisfied rules are found for the expert's conclusion.

Even though it is possible that our method of analysis might not select candidate rules to generalize for some misdiagnosed cases, these cases can be used as evidence to specialize rules for the conclusions which were reached incorrectly. This leads to an analysis of the rules for the model's incorrect conclusion that is described below in section 3.3. Finally, we note that misdiagnosed cases which do not lead to finding a candidate rule for generalization can be identified for potential changes to the case data. Such a misdiagnosed case can be reviewed to ensure that data including the stored expert's conclusion were entered correctly. In fact, cases for which the stored expert's conclusion was found to be incorrect actually occurred during the development of a model in rheumatology. A display of the performance of the rules for both the expert's conclusion and model's conclusion facilitates this case review.

3.3 Specialization: Rule Analysis for the Model's Incorrect Conclusion

In section 3.2, we described the case analysis method that led to gathering suggestions about candidate rules to generalize. In this section, we describe the methods to determine candidate rules to specialize. We need to collect statistics about rules which were inappropriately satisfied in a misdiagnosed case. Procedures are first applied to determine those rules responsible for reaching incorrect conclusions in the case, and second, to derive a measure of *closeness* in correcting the case if these rules were forced to not be satisfied.

55

By definition, a case is misdiagnosed by the model when the model's (strongest) conclusion does not match the expert's conclusion stored with the case. The problem with determining specialization experiments is two-fold: how to determine which rules should be candidate rules to specialize; and, how to determine a specific change (e.g., adding a component which strengthens a rule's conditions) after a candidate rule to specialize has been identified.

3.3.1 Choosing Candidate Rules to Specialize

To determine candidate rules to specialize, we must identify all conclusions reached by the model which override the model's confidence in the expert's conclusion. The problem is that a single rule change is often not enough to correct the case. It is not uncommon to find multiple problems with the rules because more than one conclusion was reached with confidence exceeding that for the expert's conclusion. Because of this we separate these conclusions into two classes that correspond to two classes of specialization: *primary* and *secondary* specialization. Primary specialization corresponds only to the model's incorrect conclusion reached with greatest certainty among all conclusions. The class called secondary specialization contains all other incorrect conclusions. Rules that reach the conclusions in these two classes are analyzed to obtain statistics about their performance in the case.

As an example, case 14 is a misdiagnosed case that was used to describe the case analysis method for generalizing rules in section 3.2 (see Figure 3-1). In case 14, the model's confidence in the expert's conclusion of mixed connective tissue disease is *possible* which is overridden by the model's conclusion of probable rheumatoid arthritis. Rule 66 is responsible for this incorrect conclusion and is shown in Figure 3-8. No other conclusions were reached by the model in this case. Thus the class of *primary* specialization contains the conclusion of rheumatoid arthritis, and the class of *secondary* specialization is empty for case 14.

Rule 66:   2 or more Majors for RA (MJRA) (2 Majors Satisfied)
               2 or more Minors for RA (MNRA) (2 Minors Satisfied)
               No Exclusion 1 for Probable RA (ER101) (Satisfied)
               --> Probable Rheumatoid arthritis (RA)

Figure 3-8:   Rule Responsible for Reaching an Incorrect Conclusion

We would like to determine the effect on the performance of case 14 by specializing rule 66, which is responsible for the model's incorrect conclusion of probable rheumatoid arthritis. If we force rule 66 to be not satisfied (and regardless of what is done to specialize it), then how *close* is the case to being correctly diagnosed?

To get an answer, we need to know the number of incorrect conclusions reached by the model and the number of rules satisfied for each of these conclusions. The *primary* and *secondary* classes of specialization are the sources from which this information is obtained. The rules that reach the conclusions in these two classes are traced to determine the number of rules which were satisfied, and they override the model's confidence in the expert's conclusion (i.e., those rules that conclude the model's conclusion noted by *primary* specialization, and those rules which were satisfied but not directly responsible for the model's incorrect conclusion, in the class of *secondary* specialization.)

For our example, rules that conclude rheumatoid arthritis are traced to determine the number of rules satisfied in case 14. There is only one rule (rule 66) for rheumatoid arthritis, and it is identified for *primary* specialization. If conclusions other than rheumatoid arthritis were reached in the case with confidence exceeding the *possible* level (for mixed connective tissue disease), then the rules that reach these conclusions would be identified for *secondary* specialization. The summary of this rule analysis is shown in Figure 3-9.

	Conclusion	Number of satisfied rules
Primary	rheumatoid arthritis	1 (rule 66)
Secondary	none	0

Figure 3-9: Candidate Rules for Specialization in Case 14

From the results shown in Figure 3-9, we can determine how *close* the model would be to reaching the expert's conclusion in case 14 if the rule for the model's conclusion (rule 66) is not satisfied. An interpretation of *how close to correcting the case* is associated with rule 66 that is based on the number of conclusions reached with confidence exceeding that for the expert's conclusion and the number of satisfied rules for the model's conclusion. This is shown in the table in Figure 3-10. This *closeness measure* which is assigned to a rule is not a specific value such as the percentage of total satisfaction (see section 3.2) used in determining a candidate rule to generalize, but rather it is a fixed interpretation selected from the choices available.

How close to correct?	Number of incorrect conclusions reached	Number of rules for model's conclusion
a) "will correct now"	1 conclusion	1 rule
b) "will be closer now"	1 conclusion	>1 rule
c) "will not correct now"	>1 conclusion	>1 rule

Figure 3-10: Closeness Measures for Specialization

There are three closeness measures for specialization that are associated with the rules, which reach the conclusions in the classes of *primary* and *secondary* specialization. This is done in the following way. For *primary* specialization, the single rule responsible for the model's conclusion gets closeness measure **(a)** or **(b)**, shown in Figure 3-10. We assign measure **(a)** or **(b)** to this rule because it is the strongest satisfied rule and forcing this rule to be not satisfied would, at all times, improve the chances of correcting the case. Whether or not the case would be corrected is determined from the number of conclusions reached and the number of rules satisfied for each conclusion. In our example, rule 66 gets measure **(a)** because it is the only rule for the model's conclusion, and there are no rules for other conclusions that override the model's certainty in the expert's conclusion. If there is more than one satisfied rule for the model's conclusion (in the class of *primary* specialization) then these rules get closeness measure **(b)** or **(c)**, shown in Figure 3-10. This is done because these rules were satisfied in a misdiagnosed case although they were not directly responsible for the incorrect diagnosis.

For *secondary* specialization, those rules found to be satisfied for conclusions other than the model's conclusion get closeness measure **(c)** because these rules reach conclusions in *secondary* specialization that were overridden by other conclusions (in particular, the model's conclusion). Forcing these rules to be not satisfied would still require specialization changes to other rules. After associating the closeness measures to the rules for *primary* and *secondary* specialization, information supporting the specialization of the rule is recorded with each rule. This includes the identification number of the case and the expert's conclusion for the case.

3.3.2 Determining a Component to Specialize

The second problem is to determine a specific component to be modified after a rule is identified for specialization. The statistics about primary and secondary specialization are not enough to determine a specific experiment. For instance, information about which component to add to a rule is not readily obtained for a specialization experiment as it is for generalization (to determine a component to remove from a rule). Case analysis of a candidate rule for specialization reveals only that the rule was satisfied. There is no clue as to how the rule should be modified so that it will not be satisfied. Knowledge of the types of components (e.g., majors, minors, requirements) that can appear in a rule can help in focusing on a component to specialize. A preference in changing one component over another that is based on an intuitive understanding of the components in a tabular model can identify a specific component in the rule to specialize. Frequency data about a component on the entire data base of cases is another source of information that helps in determining a component to add to a rule. These frequency data and the preference ordering are used by the heuristic rules for suggesting specialization experiments and are described in Chapter 4.

3.3.3 Summary: Rule Analysis for the Model's Incorrect Conclusion

Each misdiagnosed case is analyzed to determine candidate rules to specialize. This involves counting the number of conclusions reached by the model and the number of rules satisfied for each of these conclusions. The results of this analysis indicate a rule's class of specialization (i.e., primary or secondary), and an interpretation of *closeness* to correcting a case is associated with the rule for the model's incorrect conclusion. Figure 3-11 describes the information used in this analysis.

It should be noted that during an execution of a case by EXPERT, the tabular model for each diagnostic conclusion is evaluated in the order of entry as specified by the model designer within the SEEK editor. This allows the model designer to know in advance how to order tabular models which may depend on results obtained from the evaluation of other tabular models. For example, a table for one diagnostic conclusion may have a major component, which itself is a tabular model and, therefore, should be evaluated prior to any references made to it. Also, the rules for each diagnostic conclusion are evaluated in the order of increasing confidence levels and as specified by their order of entry into a particular confidence level. In the case of multiple rules that are satisfied for the same conclusion and at the same confidence level, the satisfied rule with highest order entry is identified as responsible for reaching the conclusion. This holds for each table evaluated by EXPERT, thus providing a uniform analysis of the rules within each table.

1. how many conclusions were reached?

2. for each conclusion reached and beginning with the "model's conclusion"

    a.   how many rules were satisfied?

    b.   if there was more than one satisfied rule, then how many of these rules
        had confidence which blocked the model's confidence in the expert's
        conclusion?

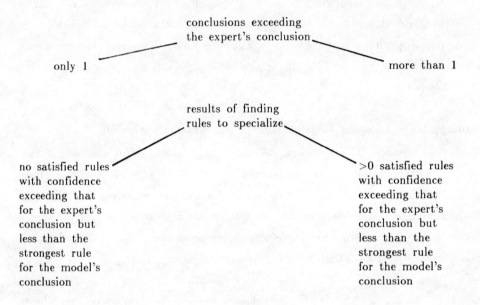

Figure 3-11:   Determining Rules to Specialize for the Model's Conclusion

3.4 Discussion and Performance Statistics

In sections 3.2 and 3.3, we described and illustrated the methods of case analysis for collecting information to determine the generalization and specialization of rules on each misdiagnosed case. The suggestions consisting of candidate rules to generalize and to specialize are compiled in the form of statistics over all misdiagnosed cases in the data base. Thus the result for a rule may consist of several cases, some of which explicitly support the generalization of the rule, and others which support the specialization of the rule. How this empirical evidence is put to use is a critical decision in the process of generating rule refinement experiments. For any rule which has evidence supporting its refinement, we want to suggest an experiment that will potentially repair as many of the misdiagnosed cases supporting the rule's modification. Because of this, the evidence supporting the generalization and specialization of the rule are *summarized* to easily identify a direction to pursue, either to generalize or to specialize the rule. These summarized suggestions are described below.

Note that this discussion has dealt with the statistics derived from an analysis of misdiagnosed cases. There is one procedure performed on correctly diagnosed cases. The rule for the expert's conclusion that is responsible for correctly diagnosing a case is marked as being used successfully in the case. Further, this rule is marked as being *significant* when the following condition holds: if the rule for the expert's conclusion was not satisfied, then the case would be misdiagnosed.

The statistics listed below about the performance of all of the rules in a model are used to suggest advise about rule refinement. The statistics with numeric labels 1, 2, 3, and 8 in this list, are *exact* statistics about the performance of a rule. They indicate current performance of the rule. The statistics with labels 4 through 7 are inexact statistics in that heuristic procedures were applied to *predict* the kind of changes (i.e., generalization or specialization) for the rules.

1. The number of cases in which the rule was used successfully. In each of these cases, this means the rule was used to reach the expert's correct conclusion. It had the greatest certainty among all conclusions reached by the model.

2. The number of cases in which the rule was used incorrectly. In each of these cases, the rule was responsible for the model's incorrect conclusion.

3. The number of cases in which the rule was significant for making the correct diagnosis. In each of these cases, if the rule was not satisfied, then the case would be incorrectly diagnosed by the model. The actual numeric value for this statistic is always less than or equal to the numeric value for the first statistic above, #1.

4. The number of cases suggesting the generalization of the rule. In each of these cases, if the rule had been satisfied, then the case would be correctly diagnosed by the model.

5. The number of cases suggesting the specialization of the rule with the effect of correctly diagnosing each of these cases if the rule is not satisfied.

6. The number of cases suggesting the specialization of the rule with the effect of moving closer to correctly diagnosing each of these cases if the rule is not satisfied.

7. The number of cases suggesting the secondary specialization of the rule with the effect of not directly correcting each of these cases if the rule is not satisfied. The rule was not responsible for the incorrect diagnosis but was satisfied with confidence that was greater than (or equal to) that for the expert's conclusion.

8. The number of cases for which no candidate rule for generalization was found, and this rule was satisfied for the expert's conclusion. In each of these cases, the confidence for the expert's conclusion was greater than zero, but no rules were found to be generalized.

We focus on four of these statistics in order to get a better understanding of th potential effects of either generalizing or specializing a rule in the model. The secon statistic through the fifth statistic are labeled respectively as G(LOSS), S(LOSS), G(GAIN) and S(GAIN) where G indicates generalization and S indicates specialization. A tradeoff i terms of the performance on the cases as a result of either the generalization o specialization of a rule is shown below. The row for generalization in the table says tha the potential gain is G(GAIN) cases while the loss will be at least G(LOSS) cases (i.e. those cases already misdiagnosed by the rule and possibly more cases depending on th specific refinement of the rule). The actual effect is determined by trying an experimen that incorporates a specific refinement of the rule.

Class of Change	Gain	Loss
Generalization (if satisfied)	G(GAIN) (at most)	G(LOSS) (at least)
Specialization (if not satisfied)	S(GAIN) (at least)	S(LOSS) (at most)

Figure 3-12:   Effect in Case Performance by Changing a Rule

The four statistics labeled G(GAIN), G(LOSS), S(GAIN), and S(LOSS) provide a basis for determining the type of change (i.e., generalization, specialization) that may be done to a rule. For instance, if the number of cases suggesting the generalization of a rule is greater than the number of cases suggesting the (primary) specialization of the rule then one should consider refinements which generalize the rule. Missing from these summarizing statistics is knowledge of what to change in a rule beyond the classification of generalization or specialization. To assist in this process, functions are available to determine if certain components exist in a rule, and to find specific information which supports the generalization or specialization of rules. For instance, there is a function for selecting the *most frequently unsatisfied component* in the cases supporting the generalization of a rule. This leads to a discussion of the heuristics for suggesting experiments.

4. Generation of Rule Refinement Experiments

4.1 Introduction

The previous chapter discussed how performance statistics are gathered about the rules in a tabular model. A trace of the rules in a case was analyzed to determine two types of statistics. We gave statistics indicating a rule's *exact* or raw performance, for example, the number of cases in which the rule was satisfied. A second type of statistic was used to *predict* a modification of the rule. For instance, when the model incorrectly diagnoses a case, two case analysis methods are applied on the model's rules to determine candidate rules to generalize and to specialize, respectively. All of the statistics about a rule's performance are accessed by functions which instantiate heuristic rules prior to evaluation.

In this chapter, we describe the heuristics incorporated in SEEK. Examples are given that demonstrate how the performance statistics are put to use in suggesting rule refinement experiments. Figure 4-1 shows the kinds of experiments that may be suggested. These experiments are organized according to the class of refinement (i.e., generalization or specialization) and the item to change (e.g., number of majors, requirement.) The heuristics described in this chapter were found useful in our experiences in developing expert models. The conditions specified in the heuristic rules are not to be construed as complete or unchangable. They can be augmented or changed.

Item to change	Generalization	Specialization
Confidence level	increase	decrease
Number of majors	decrease	increase
Number of minors	decrease	increase
Requirement	weaken	strengthen
Exclusion	strengthen	weaken

Figure 4-1: Classification of Experiments

4.2 Changing Confidence Levels in a Rule

This is an easy experiment to try. It simply means that a rule's confidence is to be changed from its current level to some other level. For instance, hypothetical rules R1 and R2 are shown where rule R2 is the result of decreasing the confidence for rule R1 from probable to possible.

R1:	R2:
M majors	M majors
N minors	N minors
Requirement	Requirement
No Exclusion	No Exclusion
--> **Probable** conclusion	--> **Possible** conclusion

In contrast to the reasoning that is potentially involved in determining changes to a rule's conditions (e.g., increasing the number of majors or strengthening the requirement in the rule), changing a rule's confidence is a straight-forward modification. We will describe two heuristics which suggest the experiments to decrease and to increase a rule's confidence, respectively. The conditions which must be satisfied to suggest these experiments are discussed, and examples are given.

4.2.1 Decreasing a Rule's Confidence

Consider case 14 which was used to illustrate the case analysis methods in Chapter 3. In Figure 4-2, the model assigned the confidence of *possible* to the expert's conclusion of mixed connective tissue disease, and rule 89 was responsible for reaching this conclusion. The model's incorrect conclusion was rheumatoid arthritis with an assigned confidence of *probable*. In this case, rule 66 was responsible for concluding incorrectly rheumatoid arthritis, and no other conclusions were reached by the model.

The recognition of a particular rule which is responsible for reaching an incorrect conclusion is required to consider an experiment of decreasing a rule's confidence. The impact of rule 66 could be reduced by decreasing its assigned confidence (for example, from probable to possible). Rule 66 would still be satisfied in case 14.

So what is accomplished by this experiment? It would be easier to find rules for the expert's conclusion if we first decrease the confidence of rule 66. A single refinement of decreasing the confidence level for rule 66 is sufficient to correct case 14 for two reasons

CASE: 14

Expert conclusion: Mixed connective tissue disease
Model   conclusion: Probable Rheumatoid arthritis

This is the rule for the expert's conclusion:

Rule 89:   2 or more Majors for MCTD   (MJMCT) (2 Majors Satisfied)
            Requirement 1 for Possible MCTD   (RS102) (Satisfied)
            --> Possible Mixed connective tissue disease   (MCTD)

This is the rule for the model's conclusion:

Rule 66:   2 or more Majors for RA (MJRA) (2 Majors Satisfied)
            2 or more Minors for RA (MNRA) (2 Minors Satisfied)
            No Exclusion 1 for Probable RA (ER101) (Satisfied)
            --> Probable Rheumatoid arthritis   (RA)

Figure 4-2:   Example of a Misdiagnosed Case

First, there were no incorrect conclusions other than rheumatoid arthritis reached in case 14.   If there were, then the rules responsible for reaching these conclusions might be modified like rule 66.   And secondly, there was a satisfied rule (rule 89) for the expert's conclusion of mixed connective tissue disease.

The impact of this rule 89 would not be interfered by rule 66 as it currently exists. In general, this experiment may be viewed as a first step in solving a problem that could, for example, require subsequent generalizations of other rules.   In some cases such as case 14, it may actually produce the correct conclusions.   But in those cases in which this experiment does not correct the case directly, partially satisfied rules for the expert's conclusion that previously were not considered for generalization are made available after the confidence is dropped for the rule responsible for the incorrect conclusion in these cases. In other words, it enhances the potential of finding a candidate rule to generalize which contains less stringent conditions for mixed connective tissue disease.   The confidence of the model's conclusion is compared with a rule's confidence to determine which rules are to be considered for possible generalizations.   As an example, those rules for mixed connective tissue disease with confidence stronger than *possible* are included in the subsequent analysis that attempts to find a candidate rule for generalization.   This is summarized in Figure 4-3 for case 14.

When should the experiment to decrease a rule's confidence be suggested?   In case 14,

	Before experiment	**After experiment**
Model's confidence in the Expert's conclusion:	possible MCTD	possible MCTD
Model's conclusion:	probable RA	possible RA
Range of MCTD rules for generalization:	probable rules: 91, 92 definite rules: 93	possible rules: 88, 89, 90 probable rules: 91, 92 definite rules: 93

Figure 4-3:   Effect of Decreasing Confidence for Rule 66 in Case 14

this experiment directly corrects the case. We could impose a restriction that this experiment should correct all cases in which the rule was responsible for reaching the model's incorrect conclusion.

There are other factors about a rule that influence a decision to decrease the rule's confidence. An important consideration is the evidence that supports the generalization of the rule. Another factor to consider is the significance of the rule's past performance in reaching the correct conclusion. However, one must recognize that the experiment involves a conceptually drastic modification. Because the expert has already assigned a confidence which he feels is appropriate for this rule, the expert's belief in all other rules for the same conclusion might be altered if he accepts this experiment.

Therefore, although this experiment is simple to perform, we want to impose rather strict conditions which must be met in order to suggest it. The heuristic for determining the experiment to decrease the confidence level of a rule is shown in Figure 4-4. This heuristic consists of four conjunctive clauses.

The first clause checks if the loss attributed to a rule exceeds the potential gain cited to generalize the rule. This is an important requirement since it compares the "current" evidence needed for performing the experiment with evidence that could reverse a decision to decrease the confidence.

The second and third clauses incorporate supportive evidence that decreasing the confidence has potential benefits. The second clause checks if the "future" gain as a result of the rule not being satisfied is at least as good as that caused by a generalization of the rule. The third clause requires that more cases *will be closer now* to reaching the correct

If   the number of cases in which the rule has been used incorrectly is greater than the number of cases suggesting the generalization of the rule,

and the number of cases that will be corrected if this rule is specialized is greater than or equal to the number of cases suggesting the generalization of the rule,

and the number of cases that will be closer to being corrected is greater than or equal to the number of cases that will not be corrected, if this rule is specialized,

and the number of cases in which the rule was significant in reaching the correct conclusion is less than the number of cases in which the rule has been used incorrectly,

Then   *Change the confidence level for the rule from its current level to its adjacent lower level.*

Figure 4-4:   Heuristic rule for decreasing a rule's confidence

conclusion as compared with the cases supporting the secondary specialization of the rule. This clause verifies that among all the cases supporting the specialization of the rule, the rule was responsible for the primary (highest ranked) incorrect conclusion more often than it was for a conclusion secondary to the primary conclusion. Why bother with this third clause? It is an attempt to enforce a stringent requirement for dropping the confidence because of the potentially drastic effect the experiment could have on the expert's expectation about reaching the conclusion.

The fourth clause checks the current significance of the rule. A rule is significant for reaching the correct conclusion in a case means that if it were removed or not satisfied then the case would be misdiagnosed by the model. It indicates how important the rule has been, and therefore what the potential loss is. Other expressions besides the one used in this fourth clause may be used to compare the importance of a rule. For example, an expression that says "the rule's rate of significance must be less than 40%" was used during a period of experimentation with the heuristics. The value of 40% was determined from our experience in refining the rheumatology model; i.e., this would be a parameter for other domains. An approach to setting this value might be based on the expected importance that the model designer could assign. The results of the system's experience in using a value may be used to adjust a specific value.

4.2.1.1 Example

An experiment is shown below for decreasing a rule's confidence. The example was abstracted from a set of experiments that were generated for the rules that conclude rheumatoid arthritis. First, the heuristic is shown including the specific values which were used in evaluation. This is followed by a narrative statement that provides an explanation for this experiment.

Heuristic satisfied for rule 66

If **8** *cases in which rule* **66** *has been used incorrectly is greater than* **0** *cases suggesting the generalization of rule* **66**,

and **4** *cases that will be corrected if rule* **66** *is not satisfied is greater than or equal to* **0** *cases suggesting the generalization of rule* **66**,

and **2** *cases that will be closer to being corrected is greater than or equal to* **2** *cases that will not be corrected, if rule* **66** *is not satisfied,*

and **0** *cases in which rule* **66** *was significant is less than* **8** *cases in which rule* **66** *has been used incorrectly,*

Then change the confidence level for rule **66** *from* **probable** *to* **possible**.

Note that the specific values which were filled in this heuristic are shown in **boldface**. The narrative statement shown in Figure 4-5 paraphrases the information used in satisfying the heuristic.

Currently, rule 66 is satisfied in 8 cases with diagnoses other than RA. If rule 66 had not been satisfied, 4 of these cases (14,73,124,3) would have been diagnosed correctly. Also, 4 cases (71,104,60,84) will have a better chance of being correctly diagnosed if rule 66 is not satisfied. Even though rule 66 is used correctly 27% of the time it is satisfied, it is significant to the final diagnosis 0% of the time.

Therefore, we suggest to Change confidence level for rule 66 from Probable (0.7) to Possible (0.4). This would weaken the impact of the rule so that it will allow other rules to possibly correct misdiagnosed cases.

Figure 4-5:   SEEK's Explanation of Experiment

Each sentence contains information that was used in evaluating a clause within the heuristic rule. For example, the first sentence corresponds to the result obtained by the function to determine the "number of cases in which the rule has been used incorrectly". This sentence is the basis of the reasoning to support the experiment and indicates the "current" negative evidence attributed to rule 66. Therefore, one should consider possible ways in reducing the impact of the rule. Note that some information which was used in evaluating the heuristic is not included in the explanation.

For the translation of a heuristic into its narrative paragraph form, each function in a heuristic has an associated English language statement where variable slots are prespecified for particular values (e.g., a rule number, a conclusion label, a particular statistic.) The translation process is governed by the functions appearing in the heuristic rule. The specific values in a function are filled in the corresponding English statement. For some functions, the exact values used in satisfying the heuristic are replaced by a functional variation of the values. This is done to improve the readability of an explanation; e.g., this occurs in the last sentence of the explanation to indicate the rule's rate of significance instead of the actual number of cases.

Furthermore, each function in the heuristic rule is prespecified with conditions indicating if the English statement corresponding to the function is to be part of the narrative explanation. For example, a conditional print switch on the function "number of cases suggesting the generalization of the rule" in this heuristic was prespecified to be included in the explanation when the value was greater than zero. The conditional print switch can be overridden at any time to produce all English statements. This is useful in investigating *all* the details supporting an experiment.

In Figure 4-5, a paraphrase of the information needed to determine the potential gain as a result of not satisfying rule 66 appears in the second and third sentences.

4.2.2 Increasing a Rule's Confidence

This section describes a heuristic rule to suggest the increase of a rule's confidence level. On the surface, this experiment is a simple modification which appears to require little reasoning to suggest it. A simple approach for determining that a rule's confidence should be increased would be to check if a rule is satisfied for the expert's conclusion in a case misdiagnosed by the model. If this is found, the experiment would then be to increase this rule's confidence so that it exceeds the confidence assigned to the model's incorrect conclusion. Although this would be effective, the experiment could have an adverse effect on the expert's prior belief in the conditions that are stated in the rule. Moreover, the expected importance in the conditions of the rules that may already exist at the *increased* confidence level could be potentially altered relative to those conditions in the rule for which the confidence is to be increased. Because of this, we want to suggest the experiment only when it is compatible with the expert's other domain knowledge implicit in his initial choices of model design.

Rather than suggest the experiment based on surface phenomena alone, we want to determine first whether another rule could be found to correct the case by removing conditions in its left-hand side. This would mean that a rule which is already at the right confidence level is, at best, partially satisfied and therefore may be adjusted by removing components from its left-hand side. When we could not find such a rule, our experience has shown that increasing a rule's confidence is a reasonable alternative.

The method of rule analysis for the expert's conclusion described in section 3.1 does not always find a candidate rule to generalize. This is because we look for partially satisfied rules prior to selecting a candidate rule for generalization, and there may be none. The misdiagnosed cases which do not suggest the generalization of rules for the expert's conclusion would be unaccounted for. By unaccounted, we mean that no information is obtained about weakening the conditions in a rule and therefore the case would remain misdiagnosed. However, advice about rule-refinements might be generated for the unaccounted cases when a rule has been satisfied for the expert's conclusion in these cases. As an example, case 11 is misdiagnosed by the model as progressive systemic sclerosis with a confidence of definite, and the expert's conclusion is mixed connective tissue disease with the model's confidence of possible. Rules 90 and 141 are responsible for reaching the expert's conclusion and model's conclusion, respectively. This is summarized in Figure 4-6.

The important point about this case is that the analysis of rules for the expert's conclusion did not result in finding a candidate rule for generalization. In terms of refinement, one could increase the confidence of the rule responsible for the expert's conclusion (rule 90) to reduce, at least, the difference in confidence between the model's conclusion and the expert's conclusion. Obviously, a negative aspect of increasing the rule's confidence is the potential of increasing the number of false positives already attributed to the rule. Thus, one could try a conservative experiment by increasing the confidence assigned to rule 90 from "possible" to "probable".

	Before experiment	After experiment
Expert's conclusion:	possible MCTD, rule 90	probable MCTD, rule 90
Model's conclusion:	definite PSS, rule 141	definite PSS, rule 141
Number of false positives by rule 90:	n cases	at least n cases

Figure 4-6:   Potential Effect of Increasing Confidence for Rule 90

An experiment to increase the confidence level of a satisfied rule for the expert's conclusion can improve the chances that the rule will correct a misdiagnosed case. The conditions under which this experiment may be tried are stated in Figure 4-7.

If   the number of cases in which the rule was satisfied for the expert's conclusion is greater than the number of cases in which the rule was used incorrectly, and no candidate rules for generalization were found in each of these cases,

Then   *Change the confidence of the rule from its current level to its adjacent higher level.*

Figure 4-7:   Heuristic for Increasing a Rule's Confidence

There is one clause in this heuristic. Among the cases which satisfied the rule, it checks for misdiagnosed cases which did not suggest the generalization of rules. This is the basis for considering the increase of a rule's confidence. The experiment is suggested if the number of such cases is greater than the number of cases in which the rule was used incorrectly.

4.2.2.1 Example

An experiment for increasing a rule's confidence is shown below. This experiment is based on the satisfaction of the heuristic with the evidence gathered about rule 90.

Heuristic satisfied for rule 90

*If **4** cases in which rule **90** was satisfied for the expert's conclusion, but no candidate rule for generalization was found in each of these cases is greater than **0** cases in which rule **90** was used incorrectly,*

*Then change the confidence level for rule **90** from* **possible** *to* **probable**.

In this example, rule 90 is cited for refinement. The support for this experiment appears in four cases. A paraphrase of the heuristic is shown in Figure 4-8, providing the rationale for increasing the confidence of the rule.

Rule 90 was satisfied in 4 misdiagnosed cases (11,60,84,130), which did not suggest to weaken any of the rules for MCTD. Currently, rule 90 is not used incorrectly in any of the cases with diagnoses other than MCTD.

Therefore, we suggest to Change confidence level for rule 90 from Possible (0.4) to Probable (0.7). This would strengthen the impact of the rule to possibly correct these cases.

Figure 4-8: SEEK's Explanation of Experiment

The two sentences in this explanation correspond to the functions satisfied by the expression in the heuristic. Note that the four cases are listed in the explanation. From this information the model designer can review these cases by entering "single case" analysis, or he can try an experiment. The actual effect of increasing the confidence for rule 90 can only be determined by incorporating the modified rule into the model and testing it on all cases.

4.3 Changing the Number of Majors and Minors in a Rule

In the design of a tabular model, the model designer prepares lists of major and minor observations which are suggestive of the diagnostic conclusion. Rules expressing numbers of major and minor criteria can be refined by decreasing or increasing these numbers. Numbers of majors and minors are easily manipulated as opposed to determining changes to specific items that would comprise the left-hand side of a pure production rule. Because of this, experiments that suggest to increase or decrease the numbers of majors or minors are advantageous over other possible rule refinements. The conditions under which one should consider these kinds of refinements are described next.

4.3.1 Decreasing the Number of Majors or Minors

The heuristics that suggest decreasing the number of majors and minors are:

If   the number of cases suggesting the generalization of the rule is greater than the number of cases in which the rule was used incorrectly,

and the most frequent missing component in the rule is the major component,

Then *Decrease the number of majors in the rule.*

If   the number of cases suggesting the generalization of the rule is greater than the number of cases in which the rule was used incorrectly,

and the most frequent missing component in the rule is the minor component,

Then *Decrease the number of minors in the rule.*

Each of these heuristics consist of two clauses. The first clause compares the evidence supporting the generalization of the rule with the evidence about the incorrect use of the rule. When this clause is satisfied, it indicates that the rule's past performance favors weakening the components in the rule. The second clause indicates the component to change in the rule. We note that the function for determining the most frequent missing component scans the information that was associated to a candidate rule for generalization in case analysis.

4.3.1.1 Example

As an example, three misdiagnosed cases supporting the generalization of rule 91 are shown in Figure 4-9. If rule 91 was satisfied, then these cases would be correctly diagnosed. Rule 91 concludes probable mixed connective tissue disease, and 2 majors and 2 minors form part of the conditions required by rule 91. Mixed connective tissue disease is the expert's conclusion in each of these cases, but the model's incorrect conclusion is rheumatoid arthritis. Figure 4-9 shows that the minor component is missing in two of these cases (14 and 71); also, case 14 had 2 majors and 1 minor for mixed connective tissue disease. Thus an experiment to decrease the number of minors in rule 91 would be suggested with the precondition that the number of cases in which rule 91 is used incorrectly is less than three. Continuing with this example, the instantiation of the heuristic for suggesting the decrease of the number of minors in rule 91 is shown with the

Information about candidate rule to generalize

Rule number	91
Concludes	Probable MCTD
Required	2 majors and 2 minors

Cases supporting generalization of rule 91

Case number	14	71	104
Majors present	2	2	0
Minors present	1	1	2
Model's incorrect conclusion	RA	RA	RA
Missing component	MINOR	MINOR	MAJOR

Figure 4-9:   Evidence Supporting the Generalization of Rule 91

values used in its evaluation.   This is followed by a narrative statement to justify the experiment.

Heuristic satisfied for rule 91

If **3** *cases supporting the generalization of rule* **91** *is greater than* **0** *cases in which rule* **91** *was used incorrectly,*

and the most frequent missing component in rule **91** *is the* **MINOR** *component,*

Then, decrease the number of minors in rule **91.**

SEEK's Explanation of Experiment

If rule 91 had been satisfied, 3 currently misdiagnosed MCTD cases would have been diagnosed correctly.   Currently, rule 91 is not used incorrectly in any of the cases with diagnoses other than MCTD. In rule 91 the component missing with the greatest frequency is "Minor".

Therefore, we suggest to Decrease the number of minors in rule 91. This would generalize the rule so that it will be easier to satisfy.

The first sentence cites the *positive* evidence found in three cases to support the generalization of rule 91. Next, there are no cases currently opposing this kind of experiment. Note that the information in the first and second sentences was obtained from the functions used in satisfying the first clause in the heuristic. This is the basis for considering an experiment to generalize the rule. The third sentence indicates the component to change. The minors component in rule 91 was cited for refinement in most of the cases supporting the generalization of the rule. The evidence supporting this change is shown in Figure 4-9.

4.3.2 Increasing the Number of Majors or Minors

These refinements fall within the class of specializations. The heuristics for increasing the number of majors or minors are similar to the heuristics for decreasing the number of majors or minors in that they require a comparison of the evidence suggesting the generalization and specialization of a rule. The difference between them lies in the information used to determine a component to be changed in the rule once the class of refinement has been determined. For instance, decreasing the number of minors is based on information obtained by case analysis that picks a missing component, from the case data, in a candidate rule for generalization.

There is no analogous analysis of a rule's *content* during the case analysis suggesting rules to specialize. This is simple to undertand. Whereas the analysis of candidate rules for generalization looks for rules and components in rules unsatisfied by the case data, all that is essentially known about candidate rules for specialization is that these rules had been satisfied, and if they were forced to be unsatisfied then other derived knowledge[2] would say whether the case would be correctly diagnosed.

The point is that *how* these rules should be specialized so that they will not be satisfied is not discernable from the knowledge about firing these rules alone. This means that selecting a component to specialize must be based on information other than that determined from a rule's performance. The notion of *ease of changing* a component can help in focusing on a satisfied component to specialize. By this, we mean to specify a

---

[2] The interpretations assigned to rules based on the closeness measures for specialization; refer to section 3.3.

77

preference in changing one component over another according to a precedence ordering over the components in a rule. One precedence ordering that is based on an intuitively reasonable ordering of the types of components appearing in the tabular model is:

minors $<$ majors $<$ requirement $<$ exclusions

where the relation $<$ means "**is easier to change than**". For example, increasing the number of minors in a rule is preferred over all other components in a rule. The heuristics for increasing the number of majors or minors embody this precedence ordering by looking for certain relationships about the number of majors or minors in the rule. The heuristic for increasing the number of minors is stated as:

> **If** the number of cases suggesting the specialization of the rule that will be either corrected or closer to being corrected is greater than the number of cases suggesting the generalization of the rule,
>
> and the number of cases in which the rule was significant in reaching the correct conclusion is less than the number of cases suggesting the specialization of the rule,
>
> and the number of minors in the rule is less than the total number of minors listed for the conclusion,
>
> **Then** *Increase the number of minors in the rule.*

Of the three clauses in the heuristic rule, the first requires that the evidence is in favor of the specialization of the rule. Clearly, this must be satisfied for a refinement that strengthens the conditions in a rule. The second clause checks the potential loss as a result of the rule not being satisfied. This is done by comparing the rule's significance with the evidence supporting the specialization of the rule. The third clause checks whether the total number of minors expressible within the minors component of a rule is not currently specified in the component. This ensures that increasing the number of minors required by a rule can in fact be done; when the clause fails, it means that there are no other minors in the table for this rule. The heuristic for increasing the number of majors is similar to this heuristic and is stated as:

If the number of cases suggesting the specialization of the rule that will be either corrected or closer to being corrected is greater than the number of cases suggesting the generalization of the rule,

and the number of cases in which the rule was significant in reaching the correct conclusion is less than the number of cases suggesting the specialization of the rule,

and the number of majors in the rule is greater than zero,

and the number of minors in the rule is greater than or equal to the total number of minors listed for the conclusion,

Then *Increase the number of majors in the rule.*

The first and second clauses in this heuristic are the same as those in the heuristic for increasing the number of minors. On the other hand, the third clause requires that a major component must exist in the rule. The fourth clause checks that the number of minors in the rule cannot be increased, and thus it makes sure that an experiment to increase the number of minors could not have been suggested for the rule. This clause is the complement of the third clause in the heuristic for increasing the number of minors, making the two experiments mutually exclusive. A preference is expressed for increasing the number of minors over an experiment to increase the number of majors. A rule which satisfies the first and second clauses is checked to determine if it contains a minor component with a value that can be increased. If not, the experiment to increase the number of minors will not be suggested. If the same rule contains a major component, the experiment to increase the number of majors will be suggested.

It should be emphasized that these heuristics for increasing the number of majors and minors contain information besides performance to determine the specific component to specialize. This is to be contrasted with the heuristics for decreasing the number of majors and minors which obtain corresponding information about the components to decrease directly from the performance of the rule on the cases. Our solution has been to include prior knowledge about likely components to specialize, which can be changed for different kinds of models. For this reason, among others, the heuristics are represented by rules which allows manipulation of the conditions needed to suggest particular rule refinements.

4.3.2.1 Example

An example is shown below of the heuristic rule that would be satisfied in order to suggest an experiment increasing the number of minors. The heuristic rule is similar to those shown in the previous examples which included the instantiated values in **boldface**.

Heuristic satisfied for rule 65

If **1** *case suggesting the specialization of the rule that will be either corrected or closer to being corrected if rule* **65** *were not satisfied is greater than* **0** *cases suggesting the generalization of rule* **65**,

and **0** *cases in which rule* **65** *was significant is less than* **1** *case in which rule* **65** *was used incorrectly,*

and **2** *minors in rule* **65** *is less than* **5** *minors listed for conclusion,*

Then increase the number of minors in rule **65**.

This heuristic rule suggests that the minors component of rule 65 should be increased. There is only one case which supports this experiment, and rule 65 is not significant in reaching the correct conclusion in any of the cases. Rule 65 contains a minors component which can be increased from its current value requiring at least 2 minors. There are 5 minors which could be required by rule 65. A paraphrase of this information is shown below.

SEEK's Explanation of the Experiment

Currently, rule 65 is satisfied in one case with diagnosis other than RA. If rule 65 had been satisfied, none of the currently misdiagnosed RA cases would have been diagnosed correctly. Even though rule 65 is used correctly 8% of the time it is satisfied, it is significant to the final diagnosis 0% of the time. Rule 65 requires 2 minors. Rule 65 does not require any majors.

Therefore, we suggest to Increase the number of minors in rule 65. This would specialize the rule so that it will be harder to satisfy.

The first sentence points the user to the fact that rule 65 had been used incorrectly in only one case. In contrast, the second sentence means that no cases suggest the generalization of the rule. The information in the third sentence indicates the rule's importance in reaching the correct conclusion. In terms of refinement, this means that there would be no loss in performance as a result of the specialization of the rule. Finally, the numbers of minors and majors required by the rule are shown. This is the context within which a decision about increasing the number of minors is made.[3]

4.4 Changing a Requirement Component

This section describes heuristics for generalizing and for specializing the requirement component in a rule. A requirement component consists of those findings or intermediate results which must be satisfied in order to trigger the rule. Refining the requirement component is similar to changing the numbers of majors or minors in that one would either weaken or strengthen the conditions in the rule.

The difference between these two is that performance information about the specific criteria which comprise majors or minors is not necessarily required in order to decrease or increase the number of majors or minors in the rule, while performance knowledge is helpful for changing the specific items which form the requirement component. Because a requirement component can be an arbitrarily complex conjunction or disjunction, we need to incorporate in the heuristics knowledge that goes beyond determining whether the requirement component should be weakened or strengthened.

This is done in a two step process. First, heuristics are tried which determine whether the requirement component in a rule needs to be changed. Next, when an experiment is suggested to change the requirement component, other heuristics are used which incorporate performance information of the specific items in the requirement component to *refine* the experiment. The following section describes two heuristic rules: (a) to suggest the generalization of the requirement component (by deleting this component) and, (b) to suggest the refinement of an experiment to generalize the requirement component.

---

[3]We have not included the preference order--that is, the prior knowledge for changing the components--in the explanation so as to focus the reader on the specific performance information supporting the experiment.

4.4.1 Weakening a Requirement Component

To determine that the requirement component in a rule needs to be weakened, the rule's performance on the cases must favor the generalization of the rule. This requires a comparison of the statistics collected by case analysis that identify rules to generalize and specialize. A second condition is that the rule must contain a requirement component which was not satisfied in most of the cases supporting the generalization of the rule. These two conditions are expressed in the heuristic rule shown below. Note that no information is specified about the performance of the specific components that form the requirement component. This is an important point because it means that the most specific experiment which can be suggested when these conditions are satisfied is that the requirement component itself should be removed from the rule containing it. However, another heuristic rule uses empirical evidence about the items within the requirement component to make specific suggestions about the component. The heuristic rule incorporated in SEEK to suggest the removal of the requirement component in a rule is stated as:

> **If** the number of cases suggesting the generalization of the rule is greater than the number of cases in which the rule was used incorrectly,
>
> and the most frequent missing component in the rule is the requirement component,
>
> **Then** *Delete the requirement component in the rule.*

There are two clauses in this heuristic rule to determine that the class of experiment is generalization and to check that the specific component to change is the requirement component. When satisfied, this heuristic rule posts the experiment to delete the requirement component. To refine this experiment the heuristic shown below suggests a specific component in the requirement component to remove.

> **If** the requirement component that has been suggested to be deleted from the rule is a conclusion,
>
> and there is a most frequently missed component in the rule that reaches this conclusion,
>
> **Then** *Delete the component.*

This heuristic rule refines an experiment which has been previously suggested. The first clause determines if the requirement component has a rule which concludes it. If so, this means that the rule concluding this requirement component must have an unsatisfied component in each of the cases suggesting the generalization of the rule. It will follow that we then want to suggest that the component most frequently missed should be deleted. The most frequently missed component is identified by the second clause. Finally, the experiment is posted, including the specific component to be removed from the rule. This process can be recursively applied to components in the rules that contribute to reaching the requirement component.

89. Possible	15 (2/1)	42 (2/1)	47 (2/0)	57 (2/2)
(2/0)	PSS	RA	NULL	SLE
	REQUIRE	REQUIRE	REQUIRE	REQUIRE
	67 (2/2)	100 (2/0)	105 (2/0)	
	NULL	NULL	NULL	
	REQUIRE	REQUIRE	REQUIRE	

Case (#major/#minor)
Model's Incorrect Conclusion
Missing Component

Figure 4-10: Evidence supporting the generalization of rule 89

4.4.1.1 Example: Deleting the Requirement Component in a Rule.

As an example, Figure 4-10 shows seven misdiagnosed cases supporting the generalization of rule 89. If rule 89 had been satisfied these seven cases would have been correctly diagnosed. Figure 4-10 shows that the requirement component is missing in all seven cases. Thus an experiment to delete the requirement component in rule 89 would be suggested provided that the number of cases in which the rule is used incorrectly is less than seven. The structure of rule 89 is shown in Figure 4-11 and includes rule 87 for reaching the requirement component included in rule 89.

The requirement component in rule 89 is labeled RS102 which is reached by rule 87. The instantiation of the heuristic for suggesting the removal of the requirement component in rule 89 is shown below with the values used in its evaluation. This is followed by a narrative paraphrase of this heuristic supporting the experiment. An example showing the refinement of this experiment that selects a specific component in rule 87 for deletion is described in the next section.

Rule 87: RNP antibody (imm.) (RNP)
positive ENA, Med titer (ENAM)
--> Requirement 1 for Possible MCTD (RS102)

Rule 89: 2 or more Majors for MCTD (MJMCT) (2 Majors Satisfied)
Requirement 1 for Possible MCTD (RS102) (Not Satisfied)
--> Possible Mixed connective tissue disease (MCTD)

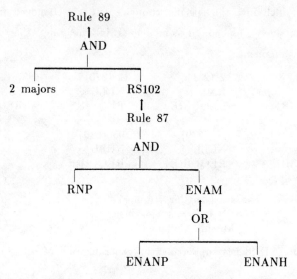

Figure 4-11: Graphical Representation of Rules

Heuristic satisfied for rule 89

If **7** *cases suggesting the generalization of rule 89 is greater than* **0** *cases in which rule* **89** *was used incorrectly,*

and the most frequent missing component in rule **89** *is the* **REQUIREMENT** *component,*

Then, delete the requirement component in rule **89.**

If rule 89 had been satisfied, 7 currently misdiagnosed MCTD cases would have been diagnosed correctly. Currently, rule 89 is not used incorrectly in any of the cases with diagnoses other than MCTD. In rule 89 the component missing with the greatest frequency is "Requirement".

Therefore, we suggest to Delete the requirement component in rule 89. This would generalize the rule so that it will be easier to satisfy.

This explanation has the same form as those shown in earlier examples for generalization experiments. There are two points to note. One is the contrast in evidence found in case analysis for the generalization and specialization of the rule 89. This is found in the first and second sentences and shows the information satisfied by the first clause in the heuristic. The first sentence corresponds to the potential gain of 7 cases if rule 89 is generalized. The second sentence indicates that no cases suggest the specialization of the rule. To determine that the requirement component is the component to change in rule 89, the information supporting the generalization of the rule shown in Figure 4-10 is scanned. An example of the refinement of this experiment is described next.

4.4.1.2 Example: Refining an Experiment that Deletes a Requirement Component

We show an example of the heuristic that refines an experiment to delete the requirement component. Continuing with our previous example, the heuristic shown below identifies a specific component to be removed from the requirement component in rule 89. In this example, the requirement component in rule 89 is identified by its internal label RS102).

Heuristic satisfied for rules 89 and 87

If **RS102** *that has been suggested to be deleted from rule* **89** *is a conclusion,*

and **ENAM** *is the most frequently missed component in rule* **87** *that reaches* **RS102**,

Then delete the component **ENAM** *from rule* **87**.

Rule 87 is a partially satisfied rule concluding RS102, and it is the closest to being satisfied among all rules that reach the conclusion of RS102. The case analysis method for selecting a candidate rule for generalization is applied on the subset of cases supporting the generalization of rule 89. The results are shown in Figure 4-12. For these 7 cases, the component labeled ENAM in rule 87 is not satisfied and therefore is suggested for deletion. If rule 87 is satisfied, rule 89 would be triggered. And, as stated in the explanation of the experiment, to delete the requirement component in rule 89, the satisfaction of rule 89 would correct the seven cases supporting its generalization. A translation of this heuristic into a narrative statement produces the explanation shown below.

SEEK's Explanation of the Experiment

Refinement for the experiment to delete the requirement component in rule 89. Rule 87 concludes the requirement component in rule 89. In rule 87 the component missing with the greatest frequency is "ENAM".

Therefore, we suggest to Delete the component labeled ENAM in rule 87. This would generalize the rule so that it will be easier to satisfy.

The important point about this explanation is that the refinement of a previously suggested experiment is based on an analysis of the cases supporting the experiment. The explanation indicates that the component labeled ENAM in rule 87 is the most frequently missed among the cases suggesting that the requirement component in rule 89 should be deleted.

In summary, we have shown an example of a heuristic to generalize a rule by removing the requirement component. This was followed by a refinement heuristic which looks for a specific component to delete from the requirement. *This process is initiated by the expert.* The expert decides whether to seek refinements of experiments and, if so, he determines which experiment is to be further analyzed. In our example, the expert would make a decision about deleting the requirement component from rule 89 or to request a refinement of this experiment.

4.4.2 Strengthening a Requirement Component

The heuristics for strengthening a requirement component in a rule are described in this section. Strengthening the requirement component means that one would add components to the requirement. Thus refinements of this kind fall within the class of specializations. This section is organized in the same way as the previous section. Two heuristics are described. The first heuristic rule determines whether the requirement

87. Definite	15 (2/1)	42 (2/1)	47 (2/0)	57 (2/2)
(0/0)	PSS	RA	NULL	SLE
	ENAM	ENAM	ENAM	ENAM
	100 (2/0)	105 (2/0)	67 (2/2)	
	NULL	NULL	NULL	
	ENAM	ENAM	ENAM	

Case (#major/#minor)
Model's Incorrect Conclusion
Missing Component

Figure 4-12:   Evidence Supporting the Generalization of a Rule

component should be strengthened.   The second heuristic finds a specific item to add to the requirement component.   As with the heuristics that suggest increasing the numbers of majors or minors, a preference ordering of components to be changed is expressed in the first heuristic rule to identify that the requirement component should be strengthened. This heuristic is stated as:

> **If**   the number of cases suggesting the specialization of the rule is greater than the number of cases suggesting generalization of the rule,
>
> and the number of cases in which the rule was significant in reaching the correct conclusion is less than the number of cases suggesting the specialization of the rule,
>
> and the number of majors in the rule is equal to zero,
>
> and the number of minors in the rule is equal to zero,
>
> **Then** *Strengthen the requirement component in the rule.*

This heuristic rule consists of four clauses.   The first clause verifies that the rule should be strengthened.   This involves comparing the negative evidence suggesting the specialization of the rule with the number of cases suggesting the generalization of the rule. The second clause checks if the potential loss by specializing the rule does not exceed the potential gain.   To do this, the rule's significance in reaching the correct conclusion is compared with the evidence found in the cases for specializing the rule.   The third and fourth clauses incorporate the condition that the requirement component is to be strengthened only when the rule does not contain major and minor components. The preference ordering described earlier favors the specialization of the major and minor components before considering the requirement component.

It should be emphasized that the satisfaction of this heuristic does not produce a specific refinement of the rule. Rather, it suggests an area that needs attention. As with any experiment generated by the system, the expert is responsible for determining whether or not to accept the advice.

Assuming that the expert takes the advice to strengthen the requirement component, then the problem is to determine how this component should be specialized. We want to assist the expert in selecting a component to add to the requirement by pointing him to the performance of components that currently exist in the model.

However, the expert is not restricted in practice as to what can be added to the requirement component. For instance, a new item could be introduced which was not previously incorporated in the model. This would require updating the cases in the data base with results about the newly entered finding, and for a large number of cases, this is a time-consuming process. While adding a new finding to the model is a reasonable solution, we would like to narrow the expert's attention to parts of the model as it currently exists which may be relevant for strengthening the requirement component.

There are usually many findings already in the model that could be applicable in specializing the requirement component. The list of majors and minors for a particular conclusion can serve as a meaningful source for this purpose since these criteria have already been identified by the expert to be important in reaching the conclusion. Knowledge about frequency of occurrence of majors and minors informs the expert about the use of these criteria. In fact, this is the idea incorporated in the heuristic described below for refining an experiment to strengthen the requirement component in a rule. Ideally, we want to restrict the selection of a component to be added to the requirement component to one which satisfies the following conditions:

1. the component is empirically consistent with the conclusion reached by the rule containing the requirement component;

2. the component is empirically inconsistent with all other conclusions.

Because of the first condition the majors or minors for the conclusion reached by the
rule containing the requirement component can be chosen as the source from which a
specific component is to be selected.   Performance information about the majors, for
example, can be used to select for inclusion in the requirement component of the rule a
specific major that has high frequency of occurrence in the cases with a stored expert's
conclusion matching that conclusion reached by the rule.   The second condition requires
checking each case with a stored expert's conclusion other than that conclusion reached by
the rule containing the requirement component.   Because this requires searching all cases
we would like to find a more efficient approach to checking for inconsistency.   We can
exploit the performance statistics available about the cases specifically misdiagnosed by the
rule, which contains the requirement component.

We can obtain the most frequently occurring stored expert's conclusion among these
misdiagnosed cases.   Once such a conclusion is determined, then the range of cases which
are searched to select a major that has low frequency of occurrence is narrowed to those
cases matching this stored expert's conclusion.

In summary, we want to suggest a component which has minimal frequency of
occurrence among the cases with stored expert's conclusion that were most frequently
misdiagnosed by the rule, while being empirically consistent in the cases with a stored
expert's conclusion that matches the conclusion reached by the rule.   This is accomplished
by incorporating frequency data about components into a heuristic rule for suggesting a
component to add to the requirement.

Given that an experiment to strengthen the requirement component is suggested, a
refinement of this experiment can be requested in order to identify a specific component to
add to the requirement.   The heuristic rule is stated as:

If   the frequency of the ITEM from the chosen criteria in the cases with
stored expert's conclusion matching that conclusion reached by the
rule is greater than zero,

and the frequency of the ITEM from the chosen criteria in the cases
with stored expert's conclusion matching that conclusion most
frequently misdiagnosed by the rule is less than 0.3,

Then *Add the component labeled ITEM from the chosen criteria to the requirement.*

The first clause in this heuristic rule corresponds to satisfying the condition that checks for empirical consistency, while the second clause checks for empirical inconsistency. Intuitively, the value of .3 in the second clause checks that a low (possibly no) frequency is needed. However, domain information may be used to change this parameter.[4]

There are two other points to note about this heuristic rule. First, the notation used in this heuristic rule needs clarification. The phrase *the chosen criteria* refers to the list of majors or minors for a particular conclusion that the expert determines. The term *the item* refers to a specific major or minor in the *criteria chosen*.

The second point concerns the evaluation of this heuristic rule. Because there are usually several items identified as, for example, majors, more than one evaluation of the heuristic may be required until it is satisfied. There could be as many evaluations as there are majors for a particular conclusion. Because of this, control of evaluation is iterative where the heuristic rule is instantiated and evaluated with performance information about each major until it is either satisfied or the list of majors is exhausted. This differs with the evaluation of all other heuristic rules discussed in this chapter for which there is only one evaluation. This is clearly an area where semantic guidance is needed. An example is described next.

4.4.2.1 Example: Strengthening the Requirement Component in a Rule

This example show the application of the heuristic rule to suggest that the requirement component should be strengthened.

---

[4]In section 4.2.1 another parameter in assessing a rule's expected importance was mentioned although not used the heuristic rule to decrease a rule's confidence level.

Heuristic satisfied for rule 138

If **2** *cases suggesting the specialization of rule* **138** *is greater than* **1** *case suggesting the generalization of rule* **138**,

and **0** *cases in which rule* **138** *was significant in reaching the correct conclusion is less than* **2** *cases suggesting the specialization of rule* **138**,

and there are **0** *majors in rule* **138**,

and there are **0** *minors in rule* **138**,

Then, strengthen the requirement component in rule **138**.

This heuristic rule suggests that the requirement component in rule 138 should be strengthened. Two cases support this experiment while there is one case supporting the generalization of the rule. The second clause indicates that rule 138 is not significant in reaching the correct conclusion for any of the cases in the data base. This means that a specialization of rule 138 would not cause a loss in performance. Thus the first two clauses in this heuristic rule verify that a specialization of rule 138 may improve the model's performance. The satisfaction of the last two clauses means that the requirement component is the candidate for specialization. A narrative statement paraphrasing the way in which this heuristic is satisfied with information about rule 138 is shown next. As for any experiment that SEEK suggests, the expert reads the program's empirical justification for proposing the experiment before trying it.

SEEK's Explanation of Experiment

Currently, rule 138 is satisfied in 2 cases with diagnoses other than PSS. If rule 138 had been satisfied, one of the currently misdiagnosed PSS cases would have been diagnosed correctly. Rule 138 is significant to the final diagnosis 0% of the time it is satisfied. Rule 138 does not require any majors. Rule 138 does not require any minors.

Therefore, we suggest to Strengthen the requirement component in rule 138. This would specialize the rule so that it will be harder to satisfy.

4.4.2.2 Example: Refining an Experiment that Suggests Strengthening the Requirement Component

In this section, we show an example of the heuristic that refines an experiment to strengthen the requirement component in a rule. The refinement is to suggest an item to be added to the requirement component. Continuing with our previous example, our objective is to show how a specific item is selected for inclusion in the requirement component of rule 138. In order to do this, we need to know the criteria from which an item is to be selected. This can be identified from the conclusion reached by rule 138.

Rule 138: Requirement 1 for Probable PSS (RR104)
No Exclusion 1 for Probable PSS (ER104)
--> Probable Progressive systemic sclerosis (PSS)

Figure 4-13: Rule Containing a Requirement Component to be Specialized

Rule 138 is shown in Figure 4-13 and concludes PSS. Thus the criteria is either the Majors for PSS, or the Minors for PSS. The system allows the expert the option of choosing either one, or lets the system make the decision. There are two other factors that we need to know about rule 138 in order to select a component to be added to the requirement component. Which cases are to be used to test for consistency and inconsistency? Because the rule concludes PSS, cases with a stored expert's conclusion matching PSS are used to test for consistency. To test for inconsistency the most frequently occurring stored expert's conclusion among the cases misdiagnosed by rule 138 obtained to determine the cases over which testing is to take place.

138. Probable 11 (3/2) 130 (5/1)
(0/0) MCTD MCTD

Case (#major/#minor)
Stored Expert's Conclusion

Figure 4-14: Evidence Supporting the Specialization of Rule 138

The cases supporting the specialization of rule 138 are shown in Figure 4-14. From this, the conclusion of MCTD is identified as the one for which cases with matching stored expert's conclusions are to be tested for inconsistency. Figure 4-15 shows the frequency data about the Majors for PSS on the PSS cases, for which consistency with the component should result, and on the MCTD cases, for which inconsistency with the component should be found. These data are compiled by the system and made available for inspection by the expert and for use by the heuristics.

	Consistency with:		Inconsistency with:	
Cases with Reviewer's dx:	PSS		MCTD	
Number of cases:	23		33	
MAJORS for PSS	Counts	Percent	Counts	Percent
SACDV	0	0	0	0
PSSBX	13	56	2	6
SCLDY	20	86	14	42

Figure 4-15:   Example of Frequency Data

Because there are three items in the Majors for PSS, there could be as many three evaluations of this heuristic. In our example, the first item satisfied by the refinement heuristic is PSSBX. This is shown below.

Heuristic Satisfied for Adding a Component to a Requirement

If **0.56** *which is the frequency of* **PSSBX** *from the* **MAJORS for PSS** *in the cases with stored expert's conclusion* **PSS**, *that matches the conclusion reached by rule* **138** *is greater than zero,*

and **0.06** *which is the frequency of* **PSSBX** *from the* **MAJORS for PSS** *in the cases with stored expert's conclusion* **MCTD**, *that matches the most frequently misdiagnosed expert's conclusion by rule* **138** *is less than 0.3*

Then, add the component labeled **PSSBX** *from the* **MAJORS for PSS** *to rule* **135**.

This heuristic rule shows that the component labeled PSSBX is satisfied in more than half of the PSS cases. While this may not be the component that the expert ultimately will select, the process of showing statistics about components currently in the model helps the expert determine which component will be selected and how those components identified as majors are used. The *Then* part of the heuristic indicates that the component labeled PSSBX should be added to rule 135 rather than 138. This is because rule 135 defines the requirement component which is used and referred to in rule 138. The explanation of this heuristic including the interaction with the expert in choosing the Major criteria for PSS is shown next.

Rule 138 concludes at probable confidence level. Do you want to strengthen rule 138 using Majors or Minors for PSS? We suggest the Major criteria labeled: MJPSS.

Enter mnemonic- MJPSS or MNPSS or Press Return for our suggestion: **MJPSS**

MCTD is the expert's conclusion in most cases misdiagnosed by rule 138. SACDV does not occur in any of the MCTD cases but also, does not appear in any of the PSS cases. We suggest to rethink whether the component labeled SACDV is consistent with the Major criteria for PSS.

Refinement for the experiment to Strengthen the requirement component in rule 138. Rule 135 concludes the requirement component in rule 138. MCTD is the expert's conclusion in most cases misdiagnosed by rule 138. PSSBX in the Majors for PSS, occurs in only 6% of the MCTD cases. Further, PSSBX occurs in 56% of the PSS cases. PSSBX appears to be consistent with PSS.

Therefore, we suggest to Add the component labeled PSSBX from MJPSS to rule 135. This would specialize the rule so that it will be harder to satisfy.

4.5 Changing an Exclusion Component

This section describes heuristic rules which suggest certain changes about the exclusio component in a rule. It is understood that the *exclusion component* consists of thos findings or intermediate results which must not be satisfied if the rule is to be triggere This is incorporated in the rule by specifying a component labeled *No exclusion* indicatin the specific exclusionary items; in Figure 4-16 the exclusion component is shown by i intended use in the rule, namely that the negation of the exclusion must be satisfied t reach the conclusion.

> Numbers of Majors and
> Numbers of Minors and
> Requirement and
> No Exclusion
> --> Conclusion at confidence level

Figure 4-16: Structure of Rule in a Tabular Model

In terms of refinement, we describe a heuristic rule that suggests the removal of t *No exclusion* component in a rule. This is a generalization of the rule, and the heurist rule is stated as:

If the number of cases suggesting the generalization of the rule is greater than the number of cases in which the rule was used incorrectly,

and the most frequent missing component in the rule is the "No exclusion" component,

Then *Delete the "No exclusion" component in the rule.*

This heuristic consists of two clauses where the first clause requires that the evidence about the rule's performance on the cases must favor the generalization of the rule. The second clause indicates that the *No exclusion* component must be unsatisfied in most of the cases suggesting the generalization of the rule. This means that the *exclusion component was satisfied* in most of the cases, and the negation of this component (i.e., *No exclusion*) is in fact missing (i.e., there were exclusions). Note that the heuristic has the same form as other heuristics described earlier; specifically the heuristics for decreasing the number of majors and minors, and the heuristic rule for deleting the requirement component.

The purpose of the heuristic rules for generalization is to suggest that certain conditions in the rule should be weakened. For the heuristic described above, the experiment suggested is to remove the *No exclusion* component of the rule. In the next section, we show an example of this heuristic rule. A refinement to this experiment would be to change the exclusion component so that it will not be satisfied.

5.1 Generalizing a Rule by Deleting the Exclusion Component

We show an example of the heuristic rule to suggest that the *No Exclusion* component should be removed from the rule. The satisfaction of this heuristic with the statistics derived from case analysis is illustrated for a rule labeled 118.

Heuristic satisfied for rule 118

If **1** *case suggesting the generalization of rule* **118** *is greater than* **0** *cases in which rule* **118** *was used incorrectly,*

and the most frequent missing component in rule **118** *is the* **No exclusion** *component,*

Then, delete the No exclusion component in rule **118**.

This heuristic contains rather weak evidence to support the experiment. Namely, only one case provides evidence to generalize the rule, while there are no cases supporting the specialization of the rule. This is not a flaw in the heuristic rule but rather characteristic of a comparative statistical analysis. This a major reason why we provide a explanation (as opposed to just presenting the specific rule refinement) of the experiment i terms of the statistics satisfied by the heuristic. The expert can make his decision after seeing the system's support for a particular experiment. The paraphrase of the heuristic rule is shown next.

SEEK's Explanation of Experiment

If rule 118 had been satisfied, one of the currently misdiagnosed SLE cases would have been diagnosed correctly. Currently, rule 118 is not used incorrectly in any of the cases with diagnoses other than SLE. In rule 118 the component missing with the greatest frequency is "No Exclusion".

Therefore, we suggest to Delete the (no exclusion) component in rule 118. This would generalize the rule so that it will be easier to satisfy.

This experiment can be refined in two ways. Rather than delete the entire component, we can pick an item within the exclusion component which was satisfied and force it to be unsatisfied. Alternatively, we can add an item to the exclusion which force the exclusion to be not satisfied. In either case, the idea is to modify the rule that define the exclusion so that it will become unsatisfied. The heuristic described below refines previously suggested experiment to delete the *No Exclusion* component by picking an item that forces the unsatisfaction of the exclusion component. This is the easier of the two approaches although a method for adding a new item to the exclusion would be analogous to that used for adding an item to the requirement component, as described in section 4.4.2. (An item to be added to an exclusion component would require empirical consistency, i.e., high frequency of occurrence, with respect to the cases with stored conclusions matching that for the model's incorrect conclusion on the cases supporting the removal of the *No Exclusion* component. Empirical inconsistency of the item to be added to the exclusion component is checked on the cases with stored conclusions matching the conclusion of the rule containing the exclusion component.) The heuristic to refine the exclusion component is stated as:

> **If** the exclusion component is a conclusion,
>
> and there is a most frequently satisfied component in the rule that reaches this conclusion,
>
> **Then** *Delete this component.*

This heuristic rule refines an experiment which has been previously suggested. The first clause determines if the exclusion component has a rule which concludes it. The rule responsible for reaching the exclusion is analyzed against the cases in which the exclusion was satisfied.

We want to suggest that the item most frequently satisfied be deleted. The assumption here is that the exclusion is composed of a disjunctive component. Our experience in writing exclusionary components is that they usually contain a disjunction of items such that a diagnosis is ruled-out (at a particular confidence level) by having any one of them satisfied. Because of this the refinement heuristic works on a disjunctive exclusion component and looks for an item most frequently satisfied. This item is identified by the second clause.

4.5.1.1 Example: Refining an Experiment that Deletes the Exclusion Component

Continuing with our previous example of rule 118, we show a refinement of the experiment to delete the *No Exclusion*. First, we consider rule 118.

> Rule 118: 1 or more Majors for SLE   (MJSLE)
> 3 or more Minors for SLE   (MNSLE)
> Requirement 1 for Probable SLE   (RR103)
> No Exclusion 1 for Probable SLE   (ER103)
> --> Probable Systemic lupus erythematosus   (SLE)

From this, the component labeled ER103 is the exclusion. The rule that reaches this conclusion is shown next.

> Rule 114: Choose 1 of the following 3:
> ..... Skin Findings: Sclerodactyly (SCLDY)
> ..... Extremity Findings: Erosive arthritis (EARTH)
> ..... RNP and ENA severely hi titer (RNESH)
> --> Exclusion 1 for Probable SLE (ER103)

The heuristic shown below suggests an item to delete from this rule labeled 114 which concludes the exclusion; and the explanation for the heuristic appears after the heuristic.

Heuristic satisfied to refine an experiment about an exclusion

If **ER103** *concludes the exclusion that was suggested to be deleted,*

and the component labeled **EARTH** *is most frequently satisfied in the cases supporting this experiment,*

Then delete the component labeled **EARTH** *from rule* **114**.

Refinement for the experiment to Delete the (no exclusion) component in rule 118. Rule 114 concludes the exclusion component used by rule 118. In rule 114 the component satisfied with the greatest frequency is "EARTH".

Therefore, we suggest to Delete the component labeled EARTH in rule 114. This would generalize the rule so that it will be easier to satisfy.

The component EARTH is selected by looking for a disjunctive exclusion component. If found, the first satisfied item in this disjunction is suggested for removal.

If there are no disjunctions, the frequency data compiled about majors, for example, may be used to pick a major item from the criteria for the incorrect diagnosis (reached in the cases supporting the experiment) to be added to the exclusion. Such an item should have low frequency of occurrence among the cases with a diagnosis matching the rule's conclusion, and in our example, this diagnosis would be taken directly from rule 118 as SLE.

4.5.2 Specializing a Rule by Changing its Exclusion Component

A rule that is a candidate for specialization may be forced to be unsatisfied by changing the exclusion component. In this situation, the component labeled *No exclusion* was satisfied meaning that a rule which concludes the specific exclusion was not fired. We can force the satisfaction of this exclusionary rule by removing antecedent conditions. This accomplishes the desired modification because if the exclusion is satisfied, the rule which references it is not satisfied. Thus, removing antecedent conditions in the exclusionary rule makes the exclusion satisfied more often. This kind of rule modification can be done in a manner similar to that for refining a generalization experiment to weaken the requirement component (i.e., by removing the most frequently unsatisfied exclusionary item found in the cases supporting the specialization of the rule.)

4.6 Summary: Heuristics for Generating Experiments

The heuristic rules described in this chapter are evaluated as the second step of the two-step process in generating rule refinement experiments. The idea is to gather data about the model's performance on a data base of cases and, to find regularities about a rule's performance that suggest experiments for improving a model's performance. The experiments are presented with explanations to the expert. The expert focuses on the experiments that appear most consistent with his domain knowledge.

The heuristic rules and their associated explanations are expressed in terms of the tabular model. We described heuristic rules that operate on the top-level rules of the tabular model, and refinement heuristics that operate on the components of the top-level rules. Heuristic rules for the top-level rules in the model propose experiments for changing the confidence level, the numbers of majors and minors, the requirement component, and the exclusion component. Refinement heuristics are applied after experiments about the top-level rules are assessed by the expert. The refinement heuristics provide a means to control the level of detail in presenting performance information about an experiment.

The heuristics suggest slight changes to the rules. However, the two heuristics for changing a rule's confidence may be viewed as not conforming to this position. The change of a rule's confidence is different than other changes that can be done, because the rule as a whole may be considered in error rather than just a component. These heuristics relate statistics that, in effect, reduce the potentially drastic change of modifying a rule's confidence. For example, relatively strict requirements for increasing a rule's confidence are specified--that a partially satisfied rule could not have been found applicable for other kinds of generalizations.

The heuristics for generalizing a rule by decreasing numeric values or removing items use performance information alone to determine the particular changes. On the other hand, specialization heuristics require other background information in order to determine specific experiments. In these heuristics, a preference ordering for changing components is incorporated, based on an intuitive understanding of the terms in a tabular model. For instance, minors and majors are easier to modify than requirements and exclusions, based on the semantics of medical tabular models of this kind.

The goodness of the heuristics is determined by the goodness of the statistics in capturing a rule's performance. The case analysis methods described in Chapter 3 provide the exact and predictive statistics with respect to the two approaches (generalization or specialization of rules) that a case may be corrected. Whether to generalize a rule or specialize a rule is determined from the summed statistics derived from case analysis on all cases. However, there is no information in the heuristics to indicate the actual impact of a particular experiment. For instance, a generalization experiment is determined by comparing the potential gain (that a generalized rule could have on the cases supporting the experiment) with the *current* known loss (that the rule has been used incorrectly.) The exact impact can only be determined by trying the experiment.

5. Sample Session with SEEK

5.1 Introduction

The purpose of this chapter is to illustrate the application of the methods described in the previous two chapters in facilitating the model designer's task of developing an expert model. A transcript of a session in the development of a rheumatology model is presented. The session is annotated with comments and is presented by sections to make it easier for the reader to follow. The model which is used throughout this session represents an early state of model development by expert rheumatologists [24]. The session includes the model's actual performance on a data base of cases. With this in mind, we present an interactive session with SEEK to experiment with the rule refinements that can improve a model's performance.

This chapter is organized according to certain stages in the design of a model. First, there is a start-up stage which gives the purpose of the session. In this stage, the model designer selects from a menu of options for testing a model and specifying conditions for evaluating the model. This is followed by a performance analysis of the rules for two different conclusions which leads to trying two experiments. The first experiment generalizes a rule, and the second specializes a rule. Finally, the refinement of a previously suggested experiment is shown.

As we will see in the transcript, the program actually carries out the experiments by dynamically modifying the rules and then reporting the results of the updated model on the cases. The model is in a compiled format which affords efficient interpretation of the cases.

SEEK is written in FORTRAN and runs on a DEC System 2060T processor under the TOPS-20 operating system. The program's runtime environment is currently limited by a 256K address space where the program consists of 100K words of instructions with the data space of about 150K words. Some of the characteristics of the program are shown in Figure 5-1. The program consists of a main module which performs the following functions:

- User Communication

- Access to Subprocesses

- ○ SEEK Editor

- ○ Tabular Model Translators

- ○ EXPERT Model Compiler

- ○ EXPERT Consultation Program

- Performance Evaluation

- Statistics Gathering

- Heuristic Rule Interpretation

- Management of Model (and Rule Refinements)

- Management of Cases

The function of obtaining a performance evaluation is critical to SEEK's interactive mode of operation. Performance evaluation involves interpreting a model on all cases. A model file is initially loaded along with the data base of cases, in the EXPERT format. All cases reside in memory for the duration of the session with SEEK and are organized by the stored expert's conclusion for efficient access and evaluation.

The actual running of the model on any case requires the conversion of case data from a packed storage representation to a form interpretable by the consultation program. Then, the consultation program executes the model on the case data. This consultation program resides in the main module of SEEK and is really a specialized version of the general EXPERT consultation system.

The runtime performance of SEEK varies with the number of rules in the model and the number of cases. Model interpretation is exhaustive--all rules are invoked for each case. In a typical demand/usage of the Rutgers DEC System 2060T with 40 to 50 jobs online, our experience on different models for which the number of rules ranged from 150 to about 1000 has shown runtime performance to vary from about 8 cases/CPU second to about 3 cases/CPU second. In building large models (with as many as 900 findings, 600 hypotheses, 1000 rules, and 200 cases,) these empirical results provide indications of the program's efficiency in carrying out the experiments in real time.

FORTRAN Implementation (15000 statements)

Size: 250K words
        (100K - Main Program, 150K - Data Space)

Cases: In Memory

Several Subprocesses
        (Editor and Model Translators)

Figure 5-1:   Characteristic of SEEK Implementation

5.2 Starting a Session in SEEK

This section presents the initial interaction with the model designer that sets up subsequent analysis and refinement of a model. The designer has the option of requesting guidance during a session or directing his own course by specifying an action from a set of available commands. The guidance is in the form of a menu of command facilities from which a selected item indicates the next action to be taken during a session. Commands have been placed on a menu list according to the particular stage(s) of model design in which they appeared relevant to assist the model designer. An obvious advantage of the automatic guidance is that the model designer does not have to know the specific commands, thus reducing syntactic and spelling mistakes. (Currently, there are nearly 40 commands, some of which require several arguments. Appendix I provides a description of the commands available to the model designer.)

The transcript of a sample session is presented next in which this guidance option has been taken. As an outline, this section includes the actions that must be carried out in order to evaluate an expert model. We assume that an initial formulation of the model exists, and that the model designer has entered a data base of cases with known conclusions for testing it. To evaluate performance, the designer may modify default conditions under which this evaluation is to be performed. There are several conditions including, for example, how to score cases in which the model's confidence in the stored expert's conclusion is the same as the model's strongest but different conclusion. We call this condition the treatment of ties for which the model designer makes a decision before requesting a performance summary. The interaction with the designer specifying conditions such as the treatment of ties is presented in this section.

{This sample session is annotated with comments, appearing in italics and enclosed in braces. The designer's line of input appears in **boldface**.*}*

@seek

-- System for Experimentation with Expert Knowledge --

Do you want assistance in this session? (Y/N) **y**

Type NOASSIST to exit assistance mode.

1. Design a tabular model.
2. Data entry: enter or revise cases.
3. Evaluate a model.
4. Search the data base of cases.
5. Describe command(s).
6. Exit SEEK directly.
Choose a number: **3**

Enter File Name: **rheum**

{The model designer specifies the name of a model to be tested. This assumes that an initial design of the model exists. If the model designer wants to enter or revise the model, request number 1 to design a tabular model invokes as a subprocess the SEEK editor consisting of a set of commands tailored to the tabular model structure. For entering or revising the cases, request number 2 invokes the EXPERT consultation program. In this session, the cases already have been entered. The fourth request invokes a data base system for querying the cases for obtaining statistical information. The subsystems corresponding to the first 4 requests are accessed at this entry stage. The model designer decides which subsystem to enter by responding with the appropriate number. In this example, the model designer wants to evaluate a rheumatology model. The response by SEEK to most model designer requests is terminated with the symbols "WAIT>" before moving onto the next menu list and is meant to control scrolling on a video display terminal.}

WAIT>

1. Enter preconditions for evaluation.
2. Obtain model performance.
3. Exit this stage of model design.
Choose a number: **1**

{These items represent the actions the model designer can request given that an evaluation of a model has been specified. The model designer wants to specify

104

conditions under which the evaluation is to be performed. Note that the model designer can request that the performance of the model be evaluated directly; in this case, default conditional values are used. The third item which appears in each of the following menu lists returns to the most recently displayed menu. The next menu list contains the conditions which the model designer may specify.}

1. Treatment of ties in scoring the cases.
2. Turn off cases and rules during evaluation.
3. Treatment of cases with >1 Reviewer conclusion.
4. Get Frequencies of majors and minors in all cases.
5. Exit this stage of model design.
Choose a number: **1**

Are ties in confidence assigned for the expert's conclusion and
the model's different conclusion treated as OK, except when
tied confidence is (0) or (DEFINITE)? Default: ties are OK
Answer Yes if Ties are OK. Answer No if Ties are WRONG. (Y/N) **y**

{In the evaluation of this model, ties are to be treated as correctly diagnosing the case.}

WAIT>

1. Treatment of ties in scoring the cases.
2. Turn off cases and rules during evaluation.
3. Treatment of cases with >1 Reviewer conclusion.
4. Get Frequencies of majors and minors in all cases.
5. Exit this stage of model design.
Choose a number: **2**

Rule Evaluation is currently turned off for conclusion(s):

None

Relevant final conclusions:

(1) MCTD   (2) RA   (3) SLE   (4) PSS   (5) PM
(6) PRAYN   (7) SJ   (8) UCTD
Enter values: (or None or Same) **6:8**

{Cases and rules for certain conclusions can be ignored in the evaluation of the model. This is useful when it is known that certain rules have (not) been adequately formulated or tested. In this example, the rules and cases for conclusions primary Raynaud's (mnemonic label PRAYN), Sjogren's syndrome (SJ) , and undifferentiated connected tissue disease (UCTD) are to be turned off and

therefore ignored in the evaluation of the model. The rules and cases for the 5 remaining conclusions will be evaluated.}

WAIT>

1. Treatment of ties in scoring the cases.
2. Turn off cases and rules during evaluation.
3. Treatment of cases with >1 Reviewer conclusion.
4. Get Frequencies of majors and minors in all cases.
5. Exit this stage of model design.
Choose a number: **3**

For each case in which more than 1 "Reviewer's diagnosis" is present, should the diagnosis reached with greatest certainty among all the "Reviewer's diagnoses" be used to evaluate the case? If not, the first "Reviewer's diagnosis" found will be used. Default answer: Yes. (Y/N) **y**

{Model evaluation assumes that there is a single expert's conclusion stored for each case. The program uses the stored expert's conclusion to compare with the model's result in order to determine if the case is correctly diagnosed by the model. However, a case can have more than one stored expert's conclusion. The question is how do we evaluate a model for such a case? We have given the model designer a simple option to indicate how these cases are to be evaluated. In a case with more than one stored expert's conclusion, we assume that each of the stored expert's conclusions is equally likely. A positive response to item 3 means that among these stored expert's conclusions, we will assign for evaluation purposes the conclusion reached with greatest confidence by the model as the expert's conclusion. This assignment remains fixed for the duration of the session. (A better method not currently implemented is to have the expert rank his conclusions for each case.) As an example, suppose a case has as stored expert's conclusions A, B, and C. When this case is evaluated, the model's confidence in each of these conclusions is ordered to pick one to be the single expert's conclusion to compare with the model's top ranked result. If the model's confidence in each conclusion is PROBABLE A, DEFINITE B, and PROBABLE C, then B is assigned as the expert's conclusion to be compared with the model's result. A negative response to item 3 means that the case is to be evaluated as a sample of conclusion A.}

WAIT>

1. Treatment of ties in scoring the cases.
2. Turn off cases and rules during evaluation.
3. Treatment of cases with >1 Reviewer conclusion.
4. Get Frequencies of majors and minors in all cases.
5. Exit this stage of model design.
Choose a number: **4**

{This request causes a compilation of frequency data about each of the majors

and minors specified in the model over the entire data base of cases. The data are saved according to the stored expert's conclusions in a file as a percent of the frequency of occurrence of the majors and minors in the cases. These data are used by the program to suggest rule refinements and can be inspected by the model designer. As shown below, the program asks for the name of the model and reports its dimensions (e.g., number of cases, findings, rules) prior to compiling the statistics about the majors and minors. We note that this request does not effect how the model is to be evaluated, but rather causes the collection of data that may aid in model refinement after the model is evaluated. It is not a conditional setting like each of the previous three items in this menu. Nevertheless, it is requested prior to the evaluation of the model to improve the efficiency of the model refinement process, i.e., collecting frequency data does not take into account the model's behavior and is therefore relegated as a task separate from model evaluation. Because of this, we chose to add this request to the menu of conditions for evaluation which is presented before the menu for performance evaluation.}

Enter File Name: **rheum**

No. of Cases:	146	–	up to	150
Size of english:	1075	–		7500
No. of findings:	151	–		920
No. of hypos:	73	–		500
No. of tables:	9	–		50
No. of chunks:	841	–		5000
No. of rules:	169	–		1200

WAIT>

1. Treatment of ties in scoring the cases.
2. Turn off cases and rules during evaluation.
3. Treatment of cases with >1 Reviewer conclusion.
4. Get Frequencies of majors and minors in all cases.
5. Exit this stage of model design.
Choose a number: **5**

{This last request by the model designer indicates that he has completed entering the conditions for performance evaluation. The conditional settings remain in effect for the duration of the session; however, the model designer can at any time revise them. Figure 5-2 summarizes the conditions under which the RHEUM model is to be evaluated.}

1. The model is to be scored as giving the correct diagnosis for cases in which the model's confidence in the expert's conclusion is tied with that for a different conclusion.

2. The evaluation of the model is to ignore cases and rules for three conclusions.

3. A case with more than one stored expert's conclusion is to be evaluated as a sample of that conclusion with greatest confidence.

Figure 5-2:   Conditions for performance evaluation

5.3 Analyzing the Model's Performance

After specifying the conditions for performance evaluation, the next step is to obtain information about how well the model is performing. This section shows how the model designer can analyze performance by interrogating the results from SEEK's evaluation. The results can be presented on a case-by-case basis or they can be presented in summary form over all cases in the data base. This latter format provides the model designer with a view of the model's performance that takes into account its overall experience with the cases.

This section shows an example of each of these two forms of results. From the model designer's perspective, the goal of this stage of the session is to focus on specific parts of the model that are performing poorly on the data base of cases. As shown below, the model designer will decide to work on the rules that conclude mixed connective tissue disease because of the poor results on the cases with this diagnosis.

1. Enter preconditions for evaluation.
2. Obtain model performance
3. Exit this stage of model design.
Choose a number: **2**

{At this stage, the model designer already has specified the conditions for evaluation and wants to obtain the results of performance evaluation.}

1. Performance results in all cases.
2. Individual case results.
3. Version of model during current session in SEEK.
4. Exit this stage of model design.
Choose a number: **1**

```
Current Performance
---------------------

            True Positives      False Positives
MCTD        9/  33   (27%)       0    (00%)
RA         42/  42  (100%)      10    (13%)
SLE        12/  18   (67%)       4    (04%)
PSS        22/  23   (96%)       4    (04%)
PM          4/   5   (80%)       1    (01%)
         ----------------------
Total      89/121   (74%)
```

False Positives - no. of cases in which the indicated conclusion was reached by the model but did not match the stored expert's conclusion.

{The results are organized by final conclusion and show the performance of the model on a data base of 121 cases. From this, the model designer wants to see more detailed results about the conclusion MCTD. An item in the next menu list allows the model designer to do this.}

WAIT>

1. List experiments about rule-refinement.
2. Single case analysis of model.
3. See parts of model or detailed performance results.
4. Exit this stage of model design.
Choose a number: **3**

1. See model parts - findings, conclusions, rules.
2. List the questionnaire for the model.
3. Description of majors and minors for a conclusion.
4. Graphical performance summary of model.
5. Performance about a rule.
6. Obtain frequencies of majors/minors on certain cases.
7. Exit this stage of model design.
Choose a number: **4**

Select one of these choices:

(Press return for display of all conclusions):

   1)MCTD   2)RA   3)SLE   4)PSS   5)PM

Enter number: **1**

```
                        Mixed connective tissue disease
                        -------------------------------
10 -
   |                                   16                    47   NULL
   |                                   26   1    PSS         49   NULL
   |                                   37   4    SLE         67   NULL
   |                    11   PSS       79   12   RA          75   NULL
 5 -                    14   RA        89   15   PSS         80   NULL
   |                    60   RA        112  42   RA          93   NULL
   |                    71   RA        116  57   SLE         99   NULL
   |                    104  RA        117  78   SLE         100  NULL
   |          84 RA     130  PSS       145  107  SLE         105  NULL
   --------------------------------------------------------------------
        OK    X      OK    X         OK    X               X
        Definite      Probable         Possible            Null
```

OK: case # correctly diagnosed at indicated confidence level
 X: case # incorrectly diagnosed as the associated conclusion
    at the indicated confidence level

{This histogram presents the 33 MCTD cases with the model's conclusion and confidence. Each case is labeled by a data base reference number. The results include the 9 cases which were scored correctly by the model and the model's confidence in MCTD for these cases (i.e., the columm labeled "Possible" and "OK" for reaching the correct conclusion, shows cases 16, 26, ..., 117, and 145.) The other 24 MCTD cases are shown according to the model's confidence in the incorrect conclusion. For example, the column labeled "Probable" and "X" includes case 14 which should be MCTD but was incorrectly diagnosed as probable RA. In fact, several MCTD cases were misdiagnosed as probable RA, and therefore they account for many of the false positives attributed to RA. This knowledge is used in section 5.6 to determine an experiment to specialize a rule. The rightmost column labeled "NULL" shows cases for which no conclusion was reached by the model. From these results, the model designer wants to look at a single case (case 14). This is presented next.}

WAIT>

1. See model parts - findings, conclusions, rules.
2. List the questionnaire for the model.
3. Description of majors and minors for a conclusion.
4. Graphical performance summary of model.
5. Performance about a rule.
6. Obtain frequencies of majors/minors on certain cases.
7. Exit this stage of model design.
Choose a number: **7**

1. List experiments about rule-refinement.
2. Single case analysis of model.
3. See parts of model or detailed performance results.
4. Exit this stage of model design.
Choose a number: **2**

Analysis basis - (1) Conclusion   (2) Case: **2**

Total number of cases: 146.   Enter case number: **14**

CASE: 14

Expert conclusion: Mixed connective tissue disease
Model   conclusion: Probable Rheumatoid arthritis

Value of Expert conclusion by Model: Possible Mixed connective tissue disease

This is the rule for the expert's conclusion:

Rule 89: Y 2 or more Majors for MCTD   (MJMCT) (2 Majors Satisfied)
         Y Requirement 1 for Possible MCTD   (RS102) (Satisfied)
         Y --> Possible Mixed connective tissue disease   (MCTD)

> *{Case 14 should be diagnosed as mixed connective tissue disease.   The model's strongest satisfied rule for this conclusion is rule 89.   The "Y" to the left of each component in the rule means that the component was satisfied.   Case 14 satisfied the two components in rule 89, namely, 2 majors and a requirement labeled RS102.}*

This is the rule for the model's conclusion:

Rule 66: Y 2 or more Majors for RA   (MJRA) (2 Majors Satisfied)
         Y 2 or more Minors for RA   (MNRA) (2 Minors Satisfied)
         Y No Exclusion 1 for Probable RA   (ER101) (Satisfied)
         Y --> Probable Rheumatoid arthritis   (RA)

> *{The model's incorrect conclusion is probable rheumatoid arthritis, and rule 66 is responsible for reaching this conclusion.   In terms of refinement, citing this rule is meant to suggest that rule 66 should be specialized to reduce its impact on case 14.   To correct the case by changing rules for the expert's conclusion of mixed connective tissue disease, rule 91 is shown below as a candidate rule for generalization.}*

MCTD   rule triggered, checking for partially satisfied rules
 >= than that set by RA   rule

There exists 1 partially satisfied rule for MCTD   with weight assignment
>= than that set by RA   rule

Rule 91: Y 2 or more Majors for MCTD   (MJMCT) (2 Majors Satisfied)
        N 2 or more Minors for MCTD   (MNMCT) (1 Minors Satisfied)
        N Requirement 1 for Probable MCTD   (RR102) (Not Satisfied)
        N --> Probable Mixed connective tissue disease   (MCTD)

WAIT>

1. See model parts - findings, conclusions, rules.
2. Performance about a rule.
3. Graphical performance summary of model.
4. Data entry: enter or revise cases.
5. Exit this stage of model design.
Choose a number: **5**

*{From the results shown about the performance of the model on the MCTD cases
and including the specific analysis in case 14, the model designer decides to
experiment with changes of the MCTD rules.   This is presented in the next
section.}*

5.4 Generation of Rule Refinement Experiments

This section shows how the model designer interacts with SEEK to obtain experiments
about changing the rules for MCTD. From his point of view, the goal of this section is to
arrive at a decision about which rules, if any, are to be modified and how they should be
changed.   To do this, the model designer first requests experiments about rule refinement
for MCTD.   Next, he selects an experiment to investigate, which is aided by the program's
explanation of each experiment.   Finally, SEEK presents the rules involved in this
experiment.   This is a systematic procedure that is carried out easily because of SEEK's
guidance facilities.   Although the model designer can request a display of summary
information about the cases supporting particular experiments, this is not included in this
section to keep the session brief.   In section 5.6, we include an example of the summary
information to help clarify the process of specializing a rule.

1. List experiments about rule-refinement.
2. Single case analysis of model.
3. See parts of model or detailed performance results.
4. Exit this stage of model design.
Choose a number: **1**

Select one of these choices:

1)MCTD   2)RA   3)SLE   4)PSS   5)PM

Enter number: **1**

{The model designer requests experiments about rule refinement for the rules that conclude MCTD. SEEK's response includes a list of the numeric labels for the cases misdiagnosed by the model. This is followed by a list of experiments ordered according to the maximum potential gain that can be achieved in correcting the cases.}

24 cases in which the expert's conclusion MCTD does not
match the model's conclusion:

1,   4, 11, 12, 14, 15, 42, 47, 49, 57, 60, 67,
71, 75, 78, 80, 84, 93, 99, 100, 104, 105, 107, 130,

Proposed Experiments for Mixed connective tissue disease
\-

1. Delete the requirement component in rule 89.

2. Decrease the number of minors in rule 88.

3. Decrease the number of minors in rule 91.

4. Delete the requirement component in rule 92.

WAIT>

1. Why do an experiment?
2. View tradeoff of cases supporting refinement of rules.
3. List experiments about rule-refinement.
4. See parts of model or detailed performance results.
5. Try an experiment.
6. Refine an experiment.
7. Rank experiments by potential ease of change.
8. Compare pairs of experiments.
9. Exit this stage of model design.
Choose a number: **1**

{The model designer wants to look at the experiment to delete the requirement component in rule 89, because it is the program's highest ranked experiment according to potential performance improvement. The program's explanation for this experiment is shown here.}

Enter experiment number:
*1

If rule 89 had been satisfied, 9 currently misdiagnosed MCTD cases
would have been diagnosed correctly. Currently, rule 89 is not used
incorrectly in any of the cases with diagnoses other than MCTD. In rule
89 the component missing with the greatest frequency is "Requirement".

Therefore, we suggest to Delete the requirement component in rule 89.
This would generalize the rule so that it will be easier to satisfy.

WAIT>

1. Why do an experiment?
2. View tradeoff of cases supporting refinement of rules.
3. List experiments about rule-refinement.
4. See parts of model or detailed performance results.
5. Try an experiment.
6. Refine an experiment.
7. Rank experiments by potential ease of change.
8. Compare pairs of experiments.
9. Exit this stage of model design.
Choose a number: **4**

*{At this point, the model designer can do several things. For instance, he can
obtain an explanation for any of the other experiments. The cases supporting an
experiment and subparts of the model can be presented. An experiment can be
tried. The experiments can be ranked and compared according to expected ease of
change. Although it is not shown in the transcript, this ranking is based on a
prespecified list of items for change that is also used to select components for
specialization in a rule. In our example, the model designer decides to continue
with the experiment of deleting the requirement component in rule 89 by
investigating this rule.}*

1. See model parts - findings, conclusions, rules.
2. List the questionnaire for the model.
3. Description of majors and minors for a conclusion.
4. Graphical performance summary of model.
5. Performance about a rule.
6. Obtain frequencies of majors/minors on certain cases.
7. Exit this stage of model design.
Choose a number: **1**

Enter finding/conclusion mnemonic or rule number:
*89

Rule 89:   2 or more Majors for MCTD   (MJMCT)
           Requirement 1 for Possible MCTD   (RS102)
           --> Possible Mixed connective tissue disease   (MCTD)

{From this, the model designer will investigate RS102 since it is the most frequently missed component among the 9 cases supporting the generalization of rule 89.}

WAIT>

1. See model parts - findings, conclusions, rules.
2. List the questionnaire for the model.
3. Description of majors and minors for a conclusion.
4. Graphical performance summary of model.
5. Performance about a rule.
6. Obtain frequencies of majors/minors on certain cases.
7. Exit this stage of model design.
Choose a number: **1**

Enter finding/conclusion mnemonic or rule number:
***rs102**

Hypothesis: RS102
Requirement 1 for Possible MCTD

Rules that conclude Requirement 1 for Possible MCTD

Rule 87:   Other Laboratory Findings: RNP antibody (imm.) [RNP, TRUE]
             positive ENA, Med titer [ENAM, 0.9 : 1]
             --> Requirement 1 for Possible MCTD [RS102, 1]

{The rule 87 can be investigated further by requesting the components labeled RNP and ENAM. Nonetheless, this rule with its conditions that are either explicitly shown or summarized into an intermediate result referenced in rule 87 corresponds directly to a component in the tabular model for MCTD. Since the components specified in the tabular structure of majors, minors, requirements, and exclusions have meaning to the model designer (he created it), the experiment to delete the requirement component contests the need for this component to reach the diagnosis of "possible" mixed connective tissue disease. Because of this, the model designer should rethink the specific conditions. Ultimately, an experiment should be tried. As shown in the next section, the model designer will take the advice to delete the requirement component. If this is not acceptable, SEEK facilities allow the model designer to obtain more performance information about the requirement component by requesting a refinement of this experiment.}

WAIT>

1. See model parts - findings, conclusions, rules.
2. List the questionnaire for the model.
3. Description of majors and minors for a conclusion.
4. Graphical performance summary of model.

5. Performance about a rule.
6. Obtain frequencies of majors/minors on certain cases.
7. Exit this stage of model design.
Choose a number: **7**

5.5 An Experiment that Generalizes a Rule

This section shows how the model designer can actually modify the rules. For each modification, the program prompts the model designer for the type of change, the rule to change, and the component to change. After entering the desired changes, the experiment is executed by running the updated model on all cases in the data base. The changes are saved in order to restore the model to its predecessor state. The result of the experiment is a Before/After summary of performance on the cases. From this, the model designer can accept or reject the changes.

1. Why do an experiment?
2. View tradeoff of cases supporting refinement of rules.
3. List experiments about rule-refinement.
4. See parts of model or detailed performance results.
5. Try an experiment.
6. Refine an experiment.
7. Rank experiments by potential ease of change.
8. Compare pairs of experiments.
9. Exit this stage of model design.
Choose a number: **5**

{An experiment to change the rules is requested by the model designer. Continuing with our example of the last section, the experiment is to delete the requirement component from rule 89. The model designer is prompted for his change.}

1. Conditionally incorporate rule-refinements.
2. Exit this stage of model design.
Choose a number: **1**

Select one of these:
(1)Change confidence for a rule
(2)Weaken a rule (decrease/delete components)
(3)Strengthen a rule (increase/add components)
(4)Insert a rule
Enter number: **2**

Enter rule number: **89**

Change number of majors or minors in rule?
(Y/N): **n**

116

Select component to weaken in rule:
 1) MJMCT
 2) RS102
Enter number: **2**

    {At this point, the program shows the model designer's change to rule 89.}

    Candidate for Change is RS102 in rule 89

    Rule 89 is:

Rule 89:   2 or more Majors for MCTD (MJMCT)
               Requirement 1 for Possible MCTD (RS102)
               --> Possible Mixed connective tissue disease (MCTD)

    Generalization of Rule 89 is:

Rule 89:   2 or more Majors for MCTD (MJMCT)
               --> Possible Mixed connective tissue disease (MCTD)

{The program runs the updated model on the data base of cases. This takes about 15 CPU seconds for this model (about 8 cases/CPU second). Since runtime performance also varies with the size of the model and the number of cases, we've tried two other models developed with the SEEK program. One is an expanded version of this rheumatology model, and the other is a model in dermatology. These models are each much larger (e.g., by a factor of 6 in the number of conclusions and findings for the expanded model in rheumatology) with data bases of 150 and 200 cases, respectively. Even with these models, the runtime performance is about 3 cases/CPU second. The point is that the program actually performs the experiment in real time, and it has proven not to be unbearably long to wait for the results. The results of the model designer's experiment is shown next.}

	Before		False Positives	After		False Positives
MCTD	9/ 33	(27%)	0	17/ 33	(52%)	0
Others	80/ 88	(91%)		80/ 88	(91%)	
Total	89/121	(74%)		97/121	(80%)	

Others

RA	42/ 42	(100%)	10	42/ 42	(100%)	9
SLE	12/ 18	(67%)	4	12/ 18	(67%)	3
PSS	22/ 23	(96%)	4	22/ 23	(96%)	2
PM	4/ 5	(80%)	1	4/ 5	(80%)	1

False Positives - no. of cases in which the indicated conclusion was reached by the model but did not match the stored expert's conclusion.

Do you want to incorporate this fix into a new model version? (Y/N) **y**

Reference label for current version: KB1.

WAIT>

1. Accept refinement.
2. Reject refinement.
3. Exit this stage of model design.
Choose a number: **1**

{The model designer accepts the refinement to rule 89, because of its favorable impact on the MCTD cases (8 cases are corrected). There is no adverse effect on other cases, i.e., no cases which were previously diagnosed correctly are misdiagnosed by the updated model.}

. 5.6 An Experiment that Specializes a Rule

In this section, the model designer focuses on the RA rules for refinement. Why not continue with the MCTD rules? A significant improvement in performance was obtained by the last experiment on the MCTD rules. And the performance of the MCTD rules is still not comparable to the performance of the other rules. Then why consider the RA rules? The answer is that the model designer is not ignoring the MCTD rules but rather, as part of the analysis that led to requesting experiments about the MCTD rules, the model designer saw in the histogram several MCTD cases which were misdiagnosed as RA. Because of this, the designer now wants to experiment with rules that apparently should be specialized to reduce their impact on the MCTD cases. Therefore, the part of the session shown in this section focuses on the RA rules that apply to cases misdiagnosed as RA when they are MCTD.

1. Performance results in all cases.
2. Individual case results.
3. Version of model during current session in SEEK.
4. Exit this stage of model design.
Choose a number: **1**

{The model designer requests the performance summary, which reflects the results of the experiment tried and accepted to generalize rule 89.}

```
Current Performance
-------------------

            True Positives   False Positives
MCTD        17/ 33  (52%)        0   (00%)
RA          42/ 42 (100%)        9   (11%)
SLE         12/ 18  (67%)        3   (03%)
PSS         22/ 23  (96%)        2   (02%)
PM           4/  5  (80%)        1   (01%)
---------------------------
Total       97/121  (80%)
```

False Positives - no. of cases in which the indicated conclusion was reached by the model but did not match the stored expert's conclusion.

WAIT>

{The model designer requests rule refinement experiments about the rules for rheumatoid arthritis (RA).}

1. List experiments about rule-refinement.
2. Single case analysis of model.
3. See parts of model or detailed performance results.
4. Exit this stage of model design.
Choose a number: **1**

Select one of these choices:

1)MCTD   2)RA   3)SLE   4)PSS   5)PM

Enter number: **2**

0 cases in which the expert's conclusion RA   does not match the model's conclusion:

1. Change confidence level for rule 66 from Probable (0.7) to Possible (0.4).

2. Increase the number of minors in rule 66.

3. Increase the number of minors in rule 65.

4. Increase the number of minors in rule 64.

5. Change confidence level for rule 67 from Definite (0.9) to Probable (0.7).

6. Increase the number of majors in rule 67.

WAIT>

> *{As was done for the experiments to refine the MCTD rules in the last section, the model designer selects the first experiment to investigate. This experiment is ranked number one in terms of potential gain in performance.}*

1. Why do an experiment?
2. View tradeoff of cases supporting refinement of rules.
3. List experiments about rule-refinement.
4. See parts of model or detailed performance results.
5. Try an experiment.
6. Refine an experiment.
7. Rank experiments by potential ease of change.
8. Compare pairs of experiments.
9. Exit this stage of model design.
Choose a number: **1**

Enter experiment number:
*1

Currently, rule 66 is satisfied in 8 cases with diagnoses other than RA. If rule 66 had not been satisfied, 6 of these cases (14,60,71,73,124,3) would have been diagnosed correctly. Also, 2 cases (104,84) will have a better chance of being correctly diagnosed if rule 66 is not satisfied. Even though rule 66 is used correctly 27% of the time it is satisfied, it is significant to the final diagnosis 0% of the time.

Therefore, we suggest to Change confidence level for rule 66 from Probable (0.7) to Possible (0.4). This would weaken the impact of the rule so that it will allow other rules to possibly correct misdiagnosed cases.

{This explanation emphasizes the "known" performance gain that the experiment would accomplish. Indeed, gathering predictive statistics to suggest an experiment is our goal, particularly for suggesting a change in a rule's confidence. This is critical because of the effect the experiment may have on the model designer's reasoning. By moving a rule to a different confidence level, the model designer's belief in the importance of criteria that are in the rules for a particular tabular model may be changed. This could be complex to resolve. Perhaps we should have chosen not to suggest experiments of this kind. Obviously we didn't, because the conditions expressed in the heuristics described in section 4.2 require knowledge of definite performance improvements in order to suggest the experiment. These improvements which are shown in the explanation are intended to minimize drastic changes in the model designer's reasoning. If the experiment is tried and accepted (in this session, it will be), the model designer should reconsider the criteria in the specific RA rules at the "possible" confidence level. Although this can lead to a reworking of the RA criteria which is effectively done with the SEEK editor. The point here is that the experiment is suggested only when the effect of changing a rule's confidence is known to be strongly favorable for a rule's performance. The cases supporting this experiment are shown next.}

WAIT>

1. Why do an experiment?
2. View tradeoff of cases supporting refinement of rules.
3. List experiments about rule-refinement.
4. See parts of model or detailed performance results.
5. Try an experiment.
6. Refine an experiment.
7. Rank experiments by potential ease of change.
8. Compare pairs of experiments.
9. Exit this stage of model design.
Choose a number: **2**

0 cases in which the expert's conclusion RA   does not
match the model's conclusion:

Rheumatoid arthritis

Rule	Certainty	No. of Cases Suggesting Generalization	No. of Cases Suggesting Specialization
65.	Possible	0	1
66.	Probable	0	7
67.	Definite	0	1

WAIT>

1. Cases which support the generalization of a rule.
2. Cases which support the specialization of a rule.
3. See model parts - findings, conclusions, rules.
4. Data entry: enter or revise cases.
5. View tradeoff of cases supporting refinement of rules.
6. Exit this stage of model design.
Choose a number: **2**

Enter rule number:

(Press return to list all rules with rule-refinement evidence):
*66

Case (#major/#minor)
Expert's Conclusion

RULE

66. Probable	14 (2/1)	60 (3/1)	71 (2/1)	104 (0/2)	73 (1/3)
(2/2)	MCTD	MCTD	MCTD	MCTD	SLE
	124 (2/4)	3 (1/3)	84 (3/1)		
	SLE	PSS	*MCTD		

{These are the cases supporting the specialization of rule 66. Case 84 is distinguished from the others with an asterik to indicate that rule 66 was not directly responsible for the incorrect diagnosis. Rather rule 66 was secondary to another rule which fired the primary incorrect diagnosis in case 84. The model designer notes that most of the other 7 cases should be MCTD. Therefore, the experiment to change rule 66's confidence should have its greatest impact on the MCTD cases; this is already known by the model designer since he saw these misdiagnosed cases in the histogram for MCTD. Nonetheless, this points out the two primary ways the program allows the model designer to view misdiagnosed cases - one from the expected conclusion (MCTD) and the other from the model's incorrect conclusion (RA).}

WAIT>

1. Cases which support the generalization of a rule.
2. Cases which support the specialization of a rule.
3. See model parts - findings, conclusions, rules.
4. Data entry: enter or revise cases.
5. View tradeoff of cases supporting refinement of rules.
6. Exit this stage of model design.
Choose a number: **6**

1. Why do an experiment?
2. View tradeoff of cases supporting refinement of rules.
3. List experiments about rule-refinement.
4. See parts of model or detailed performance results.
5. Try an experiment.
6. Refine an experiment.

7. Rank experiments by potential ease of change.
8. Compare pairs of experiments.
9. Exit this stage of model design.
Choose a number: **5**

     {The model designer will try this experiment to decrease the confidence level in of rule 66.}

1. Conditionally incorporate rule-refinements.
2. Exit this stage of model design.
Choose a number: **1**

Select one of these:
(1)Change confidence for a rule
(2)Weaken a rule (decrease/delete components)
(3)Strengthen a rule (increase/add components)
(4)Insert a rule
Enter number: **1**

Enter rule number: **66**

Select new confidence for rule:
(1)Definite (2)Probable (3)Possible (4)Null
Enter number: **3**

     Candidate for Change is rule 66

     Rule 66 is:

Rule 66:   2 or more Majors for RA (MJRA)
             2 or more Minors for RA (MNRA)
             No Exclusion 1 for Probable RA (ER101)
             --> Probable Rheumatoid arthritis (RA)

     Rule 66 is moved.

Rule 66:   2 or more Majors for RA (MJRA)
             2 or more Minors for RA (MNRA)
             No Exclusion 1 for Probable RA (ER101)
             --> Possible Rheumatoid arthritis (RA)

	Before		False Positives	After		False Positives
RA	42/ 42	(100%)	9	42/ 42	(100%)	3
Others	55/ 79	(70%)		61/ 79	(77%)	
Total	97/121	(80%)		103/121	(85%)	

Others

	Before		False Positives	After		False Positives
MCTD	17/ 33	(52%)	0	20/ 33	(61%)	0
SLE	12/ 18	(67%)	3	14/ 18	(78%)	3
PSS	22/ 23	(96%)	2	23/ 23	(100%)	2
PM	4/ 5	(80%)	1	4/ 5	(80%)	1

False Positives - no. of cases in which the indicated conclusion was reached by the model but did not match the stored expert's conclusion.

Do you want to incorporate this fix into a new model version? (Y/N) **y**

Reference label for current version: KB2.

WAIT>

1. Accept refinement.
2. Reject refinement.
3. Exit this stage of model design.
Choose a number: **1**

{The model designer accepts the refinement which improves the performance of the model. At this point, the SEEK editor could be invoked to reconsider the criteria in the table for RA, because the conditions in the rules at the "possible" level may need adjustments. This may involve changes that are as simple as removing logical redundancy among these rules or a reworking of the criteria that form the majors and minors for RA. The important point is that the model designer has knowledge of the performance of his criteria to guide his reformulation. In any event, two experiments have been tried and the results have been accepted. The next section shows the refinement of an experiment that occurs at a later point in the session.}

5.7 An Experiment that Adds a Component to a Rule

In this section, we pick up the session after a few more refinements have been made to the rules in the RHEUM model. (The specific refinements were the removal of two rules from the RA table and were done in the SEEK editor.) We show an experiment that specializes a rule by adding a component to its conditions. The important point about this experiment is how the model designer arrives at trying it. The actual experiment tried is a refinement of an experiment previously suggested. This section shows how SEEK assists the model designer to investigate detailed performance information

124

brought to his attention by an experiment. The model designer is interested in specializing rules for progressive systemic sclerosis which are responsible for incorrectly diagnosing MCTD cases. First, the histogram shown earlier in section 5.3 is used again to determine that a specialization of rules for progressive systemic sclerosis (PSS) is a possible way of correcting the misdiagnosed MCTD cases. Secondly, the model designer requests rule refinement experiments. After selecting an experiment, the model designer asks for a refinement of this experiment because it doesn't indicate a specific change. Finally, the experiment is tried.

1. Performance results in all cases.
2. Individual case results.
3. Version of model during current session in SEEK.
4. Exit this stage of model design.
Choose a number: **1**

```
        Current Performance
        -------------------

                True Positives   False Positives
        MCTD       25/ 33  (76%)      0   (00%)
        RA         42/ 42 (100%)      2   (03%)
        SLE        14/ 18  (78%)      1   (01%)
        PSS        23/ 23 (100%)      2   (02%)
        PM          4/  5  (80%)      1   (01%)
                ----------------------
        Total     108/121  (89%)
```

False Positives – no. of cases in which the indicated conclusion was reached by the model but did not match the stored expert's conclusion.

WAIT>

> {As noted earlier, the model designer must select the parts of the model that the program will work on. The performance summary shown above helps in this selection. The model designer wants to improve the performance of the MCTD cases. The same mode of investigation used in section 5.3 is applied again to the MCTD cases. The model designer requests a histogram of performance for the MCTD cases. This is shown next.}

1. List experiments about rule-refinement.
2. Single case analysis of model.
3. See parts of model or detailed performance results.
4. Exit this stage of model design.
Choose a number: **3**

1. See model parts - findings, conclusions, rules.
2. List the questionnaire for the model.
3. Description of majors and minors for a conclusion.
4. Graphical performance summary of model.
5. Performance about a rule.
6. Obtain frequencies of majors/minors on certain cases.
7. Exit this stage of model design.

Choose a number: **4**

Select one of these choices:

(Press return for display of all conclusions):

   1)MCTD   2)RA   3)SLE   4)PSS   5)PM

Enter number: **1**

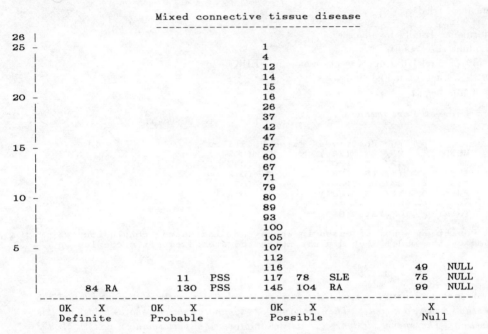

```
                          Mixed connective tissue disease
                          -------------------------------
26 |
25  -                                    1
    |                                     4
    |                                    12
    |                                    14
    |                                    15
20  -                                    16
    |                                    26
    |                                    37
    |                                    42
    |                                    47
15  -                                    57
    |                                    60
    |                                    67
    |                                    71
    |                                    79
10  -                                    80
    |                                    89
    |                                    93
    |                                   100
    |                                   105
 5  -                                   107
    |                                   112
    |                                   116                    49    NULL
    |                     11    PSS      117   78   SLE        75    NULL
    |          84   RA   130    PSS      145  104   RA         99    NULL
    -----------------------------------------------------------------------------
          OK      X      OK     X         OK     X                 X
          Definite       Probable         Possible                Null
```

OK: case # correctly diagnosed at indicated confidence level
 X: case # incorrectly diagnosed as the associated conclusion
    at the indicated confidence level

    {There are two interesting things about this histogram. First, the determination of PSS as the part of the model to work on next is shown by the two MCTD cases misdiagnosed as PSS in the column labeled "Probable" and "X". Secondly, the fact that all the correct diagnoses occur at the "possible" confidence level deserves attention. The reason for this is based on the method by which generalization statistics are gathered. The closeness measure used to select a candidate rule for generalization leads to a choice of the rule which requires as little modification, and minimal confidence to correct the case. Assuming that the cases are accurately entered, there are two situations to consider. If all the data for MCTD is known for each of the cases, then the results mean that the cases manifest the disease weakly and what may be needed now is to collect cases which are believed to be more solid examples of the disease MCTD, i.e., they presumably would be diagnosed at the "definite" confidence level by the model. In this situation, another possibility is to weaken the rules at the "definite" and "probable" confidence levels without

specific knowledge about their performance. On the other hand, if all the data about MCTD is not known, then the results are probably accurate. As an insurance, these cases should be reviewed first, to verify the accuracy of the data, but more importantly to verify that the specific confidence in MCTD is "possible".}

WAIT>

1. See model parts - findings, conclusions, rules.
2. List the questionnaire for the model.
3. Description of majors and minors for a conclusion.
4. Graphical performance summary of model.
5. Performance about a rule.
6. Obtain frequencies of majors/minors on certain cases.
7. Exit this stage of model design.
Choose a number: **7**

1. List experiments about rule-refinement.
2. Single case analysis of model.
3. See parts of model or detailed performance results.
4. Exit this stage of model design.
Choose a number: **1**

Select one of these choices:

1)MCTD   2)RA   3)SLE   4)PSS   5)PM

Enter number: **4**

{The model designer requests experiments about PSS.}

0 cases in which the expert's conclusion PSS   does not
match the model's conclusion:

Proposed Experiments for Progressive systemic sclerosis
----

1. Change confidence level for rule 136 from Probable (0.7) to Possible (0.4).

2. Strengthen the requirement component in rule 136.

WAIT>

{The model designer focuses on the second experiment by requesting the program's explanation for doing this. The alternative is of no interest to the model designer. The explanation is shown next.}

1. Why do an experiment?
2. View tradeoff of cases supporting refinement of rules.
3. List experiments about rule-refinement.
4. See parts of model or detailed performance results.
5. Try an experiment.
6. Refine an experiment.
7. Rank experiments by potential ease of change.
8. Compare pairs of experiments.
9. Exit this stage of model design.
Choose a number: **1**

Enter experiment number:
*2

    Currently, rule 136 is satisfied in 2 cases with diagnoses other than
PSS. If rule 136 had been satisfied, none of the currently
misdiagnosed PSS cases would have been diagnosed correctly. Even
though rule 136 is used correctly 87% of the time it is satisfied, it is
significant to the final diagnosis 0% of the time. Rule 136 does not
require any majors. Rule 136 does not require any minors.

    Therefore, we suggest to Strengthen the requirement component in rule
136. This would specialize the rule so that it will be harder to
satisfy.

WAIT>

1. Why do an experiment?
2. View tradeoff of cases supporting refinement of rules.
3. List experiments about rule-refinement.
4. See parts of model or detailed performance results.
5. Try an experiment.
6. Refine an experiment.
7. Rank experiments by potential ease of change.
8. Compare pairs of experiments.
9. Exit this stage of model design.
Choose a number: **4**

    *{The model designer requests to see the rule 136 which is used incorrectly in two
cases. The model designer already knows from the histogram for MCTD that the
two cases should be MCTD. Even if these cases are not known, the model
designer can see them by requesting the cases that support the specialization of rule
136.}*

1. See model parts - findings, conclusions, rules.
2. List the questionnaire for the model.
3. Description of majors and minors for a conclusion.
4. Graphical performance summary of model.
5. Performance about a rule.

6. Obtain frequencies of majors/minors on certain cases.
7. Exit this stage of model design.
Choose a number: **1**

Enter finding/conclusion mnemonic or rule number:
*****136**

  Rule 136: Requirement 1 for Probable PSS (RR104)
              No Exclusion 1 for Probable PSS (ER104)
              --> Probable Progressive systemic sclerosis (PSS)

     {From this, the model designer will investigate the requirement component labeled RR104.}

WAIT>

1. See model parts - findings, conclusions, rules.
2. List the questionnaire for the model.
3. Description of majors and minors for a conclusion.
4. Graphical performance summary of model.
5. Performance about a rule.
6. Obtain frequencies of majors/minors on certain cases.
7. Exit this stage of model design.
Choose a number: **1**

Enter finding/conclusion mnemonic or rule number:
*****rr104**

Hypothesis: RR104
Requirement 1 for Probable PSS

Rules that conclude Requirement 1 for Probable PSS

  Rule 133: Skin Findings: Diffuse sclerosis, extending above wrists [SCLER,
              TRUE]
              --> Requirement 1 for Probable PSS [RR104, 1]

    {Rule 133 is a simple rule consisting of a single condition that the finding of sclerosis must be true for the requirement component to be satisfied. At this point, the model designer decides to take the advice for strengthening the requirement. He could add a component on his own or he can have the program suggest a specific component. To follow this latter direction the model designer asks for a refinement to the experiment.}

WAIT>

1. See model parts - findings, conclusions, rules.

2. List the questionnaire for the model.
3. Description of majors and minors for a conclusion.
4. Graphical performance summary of model.
5. Performance about a rule.
6. Obtain frequencies of majors/minors on certain cases.
7. Exit this stage of model design.
Choose a number: **7**

1. Why do an experiment?
2. View tradeoff of cases supporting refinement of rules.
3. List experiments about rule-refinement.
4. See parts of model or detailed performance results.
5. Try an experiment.
6. Refine an experiment.
7. Rank experiments by potential ease of change.
8. Compare pairs of experiments.
9. Exit this stage of model design.
Choose a number: **6**

{Requesting a refinement of an experiment invokes the next menu from which several items can be selected besides the actual refinement.}

1. Refine an experiment.
2. List experiments about rule-refinement.
3. See model parts - findings, conclusions, rules.
4. Obtain frequencies of majors/minors on certain cases.
5. Exit this stage of model design.
Choose a number: **1**

Enter experiment number:
*2

{The model designer specifies the number of the experiment to be refined. The program scans the experiment to recognize that it suggests to strengthen the requirement component and responds with a question about the criteria to be used for selecting a component to be added to the requirement.}

Rule 136 concludes at probable confidence level. Do you want to strengthen rule 136 using Majors or Minors for PSS? We suggest the Major criteria labeled: MJPSS.

Enter mnemonic- MJPSS or MNPSS or Press Return for our suggestion: **mjpss**

{The model designer selects the major criteria for PSS. At this point the program invokes a heuristic rule that operates iteratively over the chosen criteria. This process involves selecting a component, filling the heuristic rule with the

appropriate data and evaluating the conditions (described in section 4.4.2) for satisfaction. As shown below, the program responds even when the heuristic rule fails and cites the component whose statistics caused the failure. In this instance, the information about the component labeled SACDV is a useful by-product of the process of evaluating the heuristic rule. The point is that although we want to find a component satisfying certain constraints, a component (SACDV) is found along the way which already has been identified by the model designer to be important in reaching the conclusion PSS but doesn't manifest itself in the PSS cases. It should be reviewed by the expert. This is shown next.}

SACDV does not occur in any of the MCTD cases but also, does not appear in any of the PSS cases. We suggest to rethink whether the component labeled SACDV is consistent with the Major criteria for PSS.

{The next response is due to the satisfaction of the heuristic rule on the component labeled PSSBX. The program links the experiment requested for refinement with the new (refined) experiment number 3.}

Refinement for experiment #2 to Strengthen the requirement component in rule 136.

3. Add the component labeled PSSBX from MJPSS to rule 133.

{The explanation of this experiment is shown next.}

MCTD is the expert's conclusion in most cases misdiagnosed by rule 136. PSSBX in the Majors for PSS, occurs in only 6% of the MCTD cases. Further, PSSBX occurs in 56% of the PSS cases. PSSBX appears to be consistent with PSS.

Therefore, we suggest to Add the component labeled PSSBX from MJPSS to rule 133. This would specialize the rule so that it will be harder to satisfy.

{At this point, the model designer must rationalize whether this component labeled PSSBX does fit into his expectation about the diagnosis of "probable" progressive systemic sclerosis. Even though the heuristic is satisfied with empirically sound reasons for selection of this component, the model designer should consider its medical relevance. Next, the model designer does indeed decide to try the experiment.}

WAIT>

1. Refine an experiment.
2. List experiments about rule-refinement.
3. See model parts - findings, conclusions, rules.

4. Obtain frequencies of majors/minors on certain cases.
5. Exit this stage of model design.
Choose a number: **5**

1. Why do an experiment?
2. View tradeoff of cases supporting refinement of rules.
3. List experiments about rule-refinement.
4. See parts of model or detailed performance results.
5. Try an experiment.
6. Refine an experiment.
7. Rank experiments by potential ease of change.
8. Compare pairs of experiments.
9. Exit this stage of model design.
Choose a number: **5**

1. Conditionally incorporate rule-refinements.
2. Exit this stage of model design.
Choose a number: **1**

Select one of these:
(1)Change confidence for a rule
(2)Weaken a rule (decrease/delete components)
(3)Strengthen a rule (increase/add components)
(4)Insert a rule
Enter number: **3**

> *{The experiment to add the component labeled PSSBX to the requirement is tried by entering the specific modification in response to the following prompts.}*

Enter rule number: **133**

Change number of majors or minors in rule?
(Y/N): **n**

Enter mnemonic of component to add to the rule: **pssbx**

> *{The program shows the result of the rule's modification next. If errors are noted, the model designer reenters his modification request.}*

Candidate for Change is rule 133

Rule 133 is:

Rule 133: Skin Findings: Diffuse sclerosis, extending above wrists [SCLER, TRUE]
--> Requirement 1 for Probable PSS [RR104, 1]

132

Specialization of Rule 133 is:

Rule 133: Skin Findings: Diffuse sclerosis, extending above wrists [SCLER, TRUE]
           Skin Findings: Skin bx diagnostic of PSS [PSSBX, TRUE]
           --> Requirement 1 for Probable PSS [RR104, 1]

{At this point, the program executes the updated model on the cases. The results include the improvement in performance (gain of one case). The model designer can reconsider the result of the one MCTD case still misdiagnosed as PSS in light of this experiment. One possibility is that the case may have errors in its data, including the possibility that the expected conclusion of MCTD may be wrong. This is easily determined through the single case analysis mode shown earlier. In this session, the model designer decides to accept the revision.}

	Before	False Positives	After	False Positives
PSS	23/ 23 (100%)	2	23/ 23 (100%)	1
Others	85/ 98 (87%)		86/ 98 (88%)	
Total	108/121 (89%)		109/121 (90%)	

Others

MCTD	25/ 33 (76%)	0	26/ 33 (79%)	0
RA	42/ 42 (100%)	2	42/ 42 (100%)	2
SLE	14/ 18 (78%)	1	14/ 18 (78%)	1
PM	4/ 5 (80%)	1	4/ 5 (80%)	1

False Positives - no. of cases in which the indicated conclusion was reached by the model but did not match the stored expert's conclusion.

Do you want to incorporate this fix into a new model version? (Y/N) **y**

Reference label for current version: KB5.

WAIT>

1. Accept refinement.
2. Reject refinement.
3. Exit this stage of model design.
Choose a number: **1**

WAIT>

1. Performance results in all cases.
2. Individual case results.
3. Version of model during current session in SEEK.
4. Exit this stage of model design.
Choose a number: **1**

```
Current Performance
-------------------

            True Positives    False Positives
MCTD        26/ 33  (79%)     0   (00%)
RA          42/ 42  (100%)    2   (03%)
SLE         14/ 18  (78%)     1   (01%)
PSS         23/ 23  (100%)    1   (01%)
PM           4/  5  (80%)     1   (01%)
-------------------------
Total      109/121  (90%)
```

False Positives – no. of cases in which the indicated conclusion was reached by the model but did not match the stored expert's conclusion.

WAIT>

1. List experiments about rule-refinement.
2. Single case analysis of model.
3. See parts of model or detailed performance results.
4. Exit this stage of model design.
Choose a number: **4**

1. Performance results in all cases.
2. Individual case results.
3. Version of model during current session in SEEK.
4. Exit this stage of model design.
Choose a number: **3**

Reference label for current version: KB5.

{The model designer has tried 5 experiments in this session, three of which have been shown in this transcript. The model designer has the option to continue, to save the results of this session, or to go back to earlier versions of the model in this session, where a version corresponds directly to a particular experiment. In this session, the model designer decides to back up to the beginning of the session.}

WAIT>

1. Save current version of model.
2. Back up to earlier version of model.
3. Ignore current session, and start new session.
4. Exit this stage of model design.
Choose a number: **2**

Enter version number or negative number to back up:
***0**

Reference label for current version: KB0.

WAIT>

1. Performance results in all cases.
2. Individual case results.
3. Version of model during current session in SEEK.
4. Exit this stage of model design.
Choose a number: **1**

```
        Current Performance
        -------------------

                 True Positives   False Positives
        MCTD         9/ 33  (27%)        0   (00%)
        RA          42/ 42 (100%)       10   (13%)
        SLE         12/ 18  (67%)        4   (04%)
        PSS         22/ 23  (96%)        4   (04%)
        PM           4/  5  (80%)        1   (01%)
        -----------------------
        Total       89/121  (74%)
```

False Positives - no. of cases in which the indicated conclusion was
reached by the model but did not match the stored expert's conclusion.

*{At this point, the state of the model is restored. The model designer terminates
the session.}*

WAIT>

1. List experiments about rule-refinement.
2. Single case analysis of model.
3. See parts of model or detailed performance results.
4. Exit this stage of model design.
Choose a number: **4**

1. Performance results in all cases.
2. Individual case results.
3. Version of model during current session in SEEK.
4. Exit this stage of model design.
Choose a number: **4**

1. Design a tabular model.
2. Data entry: enter or revise cases.
3. Evaluate a model.
4. Search the data base of cases.
5. Describe command(s).
6. Exit SEEK directly.
Choose a number: **6**

[DONE]

5.8 Summary of a Session with SEEK

This chapter has illustrated an interactive session with SEEK in refining a model. The model designer tests a model after specifying conditions under which the evaluation is to be done. First, he requests an evaluation. The results are presented and analyzed. A section of the model is identified for possible rule refinement. Second, the model designer inquires for advice about improving the performance of the model. The program replies with possible rule changes and empirical reasons why they are suggested. Third, the model designer refines some rules. The program runs the revised model on the data base of cases and reports the results. This process is then repeated.

The session demonstrated that performance information can be effectively integrated into the process of expert model development. A model's performance on a data base of cases is used to identify potential problems with the rules. Performance information is accessed by the program in the form of summarized statistics to suggest ways of correcting the problems. Finally, performance summaries aid the model designer in empirically verifying his revisions. Command facilities provide efficient examination of the model and its performance. Because there are many things that the model designer can do in any one stage of the session, we have implemented a guidance facility to simplify the selection of a particular action by grouping various commands according to the stage of model design in which they are most likely to be required. There are a several facilities which the model designer did not use in the session although they appeared as items in the menus. For instance, the editor for entering the expert's rules was designed to be used straightforwardly with commands tailored to the tabular model structure.

6. Discussion and Suggestions for Future Work

6.1 Results and Discussion

The goal of this research was to propose practical methods for building and verifying the performance of expert models for realistic large-scale medical applications. The thesis has described an interactive system that provides a unified framework for designing and testing expert models, and applied it to the development of a diagnostic consultation system in rheumatology. The implementation and successful development of SEEK has demonstrated that performance information can be integrated into the design stage of an expert model. A model's past experience in diagnosing cases can be efficiently utilized to generate intelligent advice about refining a model's rules to improve performance. Sections 6.1.1 through 6.1.4 review the main points which contribute to the realization of this capability -- *Unified Framework for Model Design and Testing, Tabular Model, Heuristics for Generating Advice,* and *Dual Sources of Knowledge.*

6.1.1 Unified Framework for Model Design and Testing

Our specific result is that advice about rule refinement to improve a model's performance can be generated in a unified framework for model design and testing. In this section, we will review the interaction with the model designer.

The basic process in using SEEK is an incremental design of an expert model. The model designer first enters his rules in the tabular model format. Then cases are entered for testing purposes. Incremental design is carried out by three steps:

1. evaluate the model on the test cases.

2. analyze the rules.

3. revise the rules.

All three steps are initiated by the model designer. He decides, for example, whether to look at the performance of the model with respect to all cases and therefore obtain a global performance summary, or to investigate the performance of the model on a single case. A more informative view is obtained from a performance summary on all cases. The bottom-line results of the model show exactly which of the major parts of the model are performing well and which are not. This eases the model designer's next step in selecting a part of the model to investigate further.

Unified Framework for Expert Model Design and Testing

- Expert-Derived Rules in a relatively simple model representation

- Case Experience in the form of stored cases with known diagnoses

- *Can Build a Real-World Expert Model* for large-scale diagnostic application

Generation of Advice in the Design of an Expert Model

- Gather Performance Statistics about the Model at the Design Stage

- *Can Generate Intelligent Advice* about rule refinement to improve a model's performance

Figure 6-1:   Research Results

To get to the third step for revising the rules usually involves a lot of work in determining which rule to revise and specific changes. It is in the second and third step that SEEK can provide great assistance to the model designer. The model designer selects a tabular model and requests experiments about the rules, and SEEK takes over to analyze the rules involved and to suggest likely changes.[5]

The extent to which SEEK is a productive aid may be assessed by considering the specific interaction with the model designer. We summarize below certain points in the incremental design process where the model designer supplies information:

1. the determination of conditions for evaluating the model;

2. the selection of a final conclusion for which rules are to be analyzed;

3. the selection of rule refinement experiments;

4. the review of the impact of an experiment.

---

[5]To say that SEEK begins its analysis at the second step technically is not true since some of the performance statistics are already available from the performance evaluation of the model on all cases. For example, the statistics about a rule's correct use and significance are known and available particularly for evaluating the heuristics. The three steps serve more as a guide in understanding the process than in indicating specific sections of the program.

The model designer informs SEEK about characteristics of the domain and about how to proceed in the design of a model at these four points. First, the conditions for evaluating the model require background information about the domain. An important example is the treatment of ties in confidence between the expert's conclusion for a case and the model's different conclusion. Here, knowledge about how conclusions present themselves in the domain is incorporated into SEEK's evaluation of a model. This impacts not only the explicit performance results but also the kinds of rule refinements that the system will generate.[6] In section 6.2, we suggest an improvement on the specification of how ties should be treated by considering individually the conclusions which may overlap and at particular confidence levels.

Another example of a condition for model evaluation is to indicate the conclusions for which rules and cases should not be included in the evaluation of the model. The benefits of this relate primarily to the practical aspects of model design. For example, when rules have not been adequately prepared and cases are not available for certain conclusions, the model designer can still proceed by temporarily ignoring such conclusions.

After specifying the conditions for model evaluation and obtaining the results of model evaluation, the model designer must select a conclusion for which rules are to be analyzed for the generation of rule refinement experiments. This is a means of forcing the model designer to think about his criteria. The performance summary of the model over all cases is the source from which this decision is made. After selection, the experiments presented to the model designer must be analyzed. We have emphasized this point at various times because it is here that the consideration of other domain knowledge is critical to obtain a medically sound set of rules. In section 6.2, we suggest a means of improving the selection of a particular experiment by generating experiments over all conclusions. Also, suggestions are presented for incorporating domain-specific knowledge into the heuristics, and thereby, potentially focus on more relevant experiments than those which rely on empirical information alone.

The last point in the incremental model design process is the acceptance or rejection of the experiments. Clearly, a definite improvement in performance of the updated model

---

[6]In the examples shown throughout the thesis, we have treated ties as correct. It should be clear that possibly very different results and experiments may appear if ties are treated as incorrect (i.e., if the conclusions were considered mutually exclusive.)

on the cases is an important criterion for accepting an experiment. However, the results of an experiment may not show gain in performance and, in fact, may cause a degradation in performance. The key criterion about whether to accept an experiment is the model designer's belief in the adequacy or medical relevancy of the specific rule refinements tried. This reemphasizes the importance of the selection of an experiment where the model designer is expected to select an experiment(s) that is most consistent with his domain knowledge. Finally, performance results on all cases aid in the verification of the model.

In summary, we have identified explicit points where certain kinds of user-specified information enters into empirical testing. Some information is entered directly and will probably remain in effect for the duration of the model design process (e.g., the treatment of ties). Other information is specified following an analysis of the following results: performance summary, the suggested experiments, and the impact of experimental results. An area for future work lies in finding ways of explicitly representing more of the background information used in the analysis of these results.

6.1.2 Tabular Model

In this section, we review the tabular model for expressing and evaluating expert decision-making knowledge and conclude the section with a discussion about the model's general applicability.

6.1.2.1 Expressing Expert Knowledge

As a tool for encoding an expert's decision rules, the tabular model provides a framework for reducing the dimensionality inherent in large-scale medical applications. A strongly related point concerns the tabular model's effectiveness for expressing discrimination criteria. To get a better understanding of these points, let's review how the tabular model is put together.

The process of formulating a table for a given diagnosis requires two steps. The first step is for the expert to list the findings which he believes are relevant in reaching the diagnosis. Even though a set of such findings can be quite large, the terms *majors*, *minors*, *requirements*, and *exclusions* are used to group findings according to their importance and specific relevance in reaching a particular diagnosis. These terms are relatively easy to understand particularly in medicine where they have been used in formalizing criteria for various diseases.

The second step is to write the rules with respect to the three confidence levels of *definite, probable,* and *possible.* An important organizational attribute of the tabular model is that all rules for a given diagnosis are expressed together and are ordered by the three confidence levels. The expert focuses on a confidence level and formulates a rule as a conjunction of these components: numbers of majors and minors, a requirement, and an exclusion. The important aspect of this rule formulation process is the semantics implicit in the components used to reach a diagnosis. For instance, while the components consisting of a requirement and an exclusion form the necessary conditions, one can think of the numbers of majors and minors as sufficiency conditions for considering the diagnosis at a particular confidence level.

The expression of discrimination criteria is an important part of rule formulation for obtaining a model with realistic performance. In terms of the tabular model, discriminating criteria include the specific requirements which must be satisfied to reach a diagnosis, and the exclusions which rule-out a diagnosis at a particular confidence level. The level of description of these conditions can be refined by expressing intermediate rules; such a rule groups or summarizes particular combinations of detailed findings which comprise and contribute to reaching a requirement or exclusion. This is not to mean that just because the terms of requirements and exclusions are available, one can easily write discriminating diagnostic criteria. This facility comes from the overall process of writing tabular models systematically for each disease and of applying the fixed types of terms uniformly. In doing so, the expert will have to consider the types of relations among diseases for determining useful exclusions.

5.1.2.2 Evaluating Expert Knowledge

Since the model's confidence in a diagnosis is directly determined from a rule satisfied with greatest confidence, the expert knows how his rules are going to be evaluated. Our experience has shown that even for an expert physician previously unfamiliar with the tabular model, the tabular scheme for expressing rules is quickly grasped.

A deterministic evaluation of rules in the tabular model is the foundation for analyzing the performance of the model's rules. SEEK can easily assess which rules were correctly fired and which were not. This has led to case analysis methods that gather predictive statistics about rules to generalize and specialize.[7]

The tabular model format makes for an efficient translation into the EXPERT syntax used by SEEK. This format imposes an ordering on the evaluation of rules--for example, rules that conclude intermediate results such as the numbers of majors and minors precede the final diagnostic rules. The model is automatically translated into the EXPERT syntax. The translation is not a difficult process primarily because simple representational structures in the EXPERT formalism are suitable for encoding the tabular model. (Appendix I shows examples of the formats involved in the translation of a tabular model.)

6.1.2.3 Applicability of the Tabular Model

Problems that can be cast as classification-type tasks may be suitable for analysis by SEEK. The practical aspect of the consultation task is viewed as a single session of diagnostic consultation, where all the case data are entered before the final conclusions are analyzed. If the problem can be put into the fixed structure of the tabular model where the relevant decision-making knowledge can be represented by production rules, then the interactive tabular model design and testing framework provided by SEEK should be strongly considered to assist in expert model development.

The tabular model may prove quite reasonable for expressing knowledge which has few deterministic logical criteria but rather many uncertainty relations with varying individual contributions to the overall decision-making. This is the situation for rheumatology. In this domain, the use of majors and minors provides a simple initial level of abstraction to separate and test the importance of the criteria.

In general, the decision-making process in a domain should be largely based on empirical associations in which the observations of the domain can be related to majors, minors, requirements, and exclusions to effectively reduce the dimensionality of the problem. In rheumatology for example, this has been highly successful where there are hundreds of observations in the questionnaire of the latest model (1982) which are manageably organized in the tabular model. Although confidence is fixed to 3 levels, this can ease the

---

[7]It should be noted that logical analysis of the model structure may be performed where certain kinds of check would be beneficial--for example, simple logical procedures such as checking for redundancies or gaps in the expression of numbers of majors and minors between rules might be incorporated as a subprocess of the SEEK editor. Some approaches to doing this kind of logical analysis appear in [31].

expert's task of writing rules, especially when grappling with diagnoses that are overlapping and not mutually exclusive.

The tabular model may be inadequate for other application areas. Encoding knowledge in terms of majors and minors may be difficult for some applications. In such domains, the tabular model may still be used where all knowledge is encoded as requirements and exclusions.[8] However, without majors and minors (or any other uniformly applied abstraction terms) and especially if dimensions are quite large, rule formulation can be quite difficult. Without the use of majors and minors there is a loss both in the explicit structure and in the implicit semantics they provide to the overall design of a model--this is critical to reduce the complexity of the rule formulation process.

For other applications, domain knowledge can have a richer inference structure than that provided by the tabular model. For instance, it may be the case that more refined levels of inferencing are needed than the three confidence levels of *definite*, *probable*, and *possible*. Also, the tabular model framework does not provide explicit links among tabular models (i.e., hierarchical or other descriptive connections). However, hierarchical relations can be encoded in the rules of a model and therefore would be included only as they pertain to decision-making in the application area. For instance, a reference of a disease as a major in one table may be defined by another table to indicate a hierarchical relation.

Another consideration about the tabular model framework is that it does not provide a means to specify control of the consultation session.[9] There is no means to indicate explicitly various questioning orderings directly in the tabular model. During the execution of a consultation, there is limited interaction between the questioning strategy and the evaluation of the model; questioning is done in a fixed order before the model's rules are tried. We have largely ignored the user interaction in the consultation session and have concentrated on acquiring the rules that are useful for the consultation.

---

[8]We note that SEEK can function without majors and minors, in which case the rule refinements would be limited to removing or adding specific components. For generalization experiments, this does not present any significant problems since the component chosen for deletion is taken from the performance of the rule in which the component is a part. On the other hand, there is a problem in determining the pre-conditions for adding a component to a rule. In the current scheme, the lists of majors or minors are used to localize the selection of an item to add to a rule. An extension to handle this is that frequency data about the items in the requirements and exclusions of the rules could be compiled over all cases and made available for the expert to inspect.

[9] [2] shows how control knowledge is made explicit in the prototypes of the CENTAUR system for improving the efficiency of the consultation session.

However, we do consider the questioning scheme an area of future work. This can be complex since, on the one hand the simple scoring function affords the ease with which rule experimentation can be done, yet, integrating control information about questioning into the model's evaluation makes empirical analysis less direct. Ideally, we would want to give the capability of explicitly indicating question ordering in the tabular model directly without sacrificing the predictive analysis of the model's behavior. One possible direction to accomplish this is to introduce another term in the tabular model which would reference a subset of the majors and minors of a given table in a preferred order for questioning. The idea is to ask the questions containing these items prior to evaluating the rules. When a prespecified number of them are satisfactorily answered for their use in the rules, the system would pursue other questions derived from the contents of partially satisfied rules to confirm diagnoses at particular confidence levels. Although this is just a first step, the idea is to make the questioning scheme more focused but relatively separate from model evaluation.

6.1.3 Heuristics for Suggesting Rule Refinement Advice

There are about a dozen heuristic rules for generating rule refinement experiments. The heuristic rules relate performance statistics about a model's rules to determine rule changes for the expert to consider. In this section, we review the formulation and adequacy of the heuristic rules.

6.1.3.1 Formulating the Heuristics

We need to review the process of gathering performance statistics to understand how the heuristics were formulated.[10]

An important consideration in the design of SEEK was to identify which statistics were to be gathered. Some of the statistics were obvious at the outset, while others were found after some experience with the program in the early stage of its development. The easy ones were derived from knowledge about the model's behavior--credit and blame for rule are directly determined--and are readily available for performance analysis. Some of the other statistics were derived from our practical goals--for generalization, to find a rule which would correct a misdiagnosed case meant to look for partially satisfied rules whose confidence exceeded that for the model's incorrect conclusion.

---

[10]Gathering statistics is the basis for all subsequent actions taken in the course of finding an experiment for improving the model's performance.

A common-sense analysis of the performance of a model's rule was applied to determine which statistics to relate in a heuristic rule. For instance, if more cases have been found to favor the weakening of a rule's conditions as opposed to strengthening the rule, then a generalization experiment should be considered. A statistical comparison of this kind appears in most of the heuristic rules described in Chapter 4.

To determine a specific generalization experiment for a rule is a relatively easy process to understand. If it is empirically known that a rule should be generalized, a search is needed on each of the cases supporting the generalization of the rule to find some pattern about the rule's unsatisfied components. Case analysis provides important information for this, namely, the first unsatisfied component found in the rule. Because of this, all that is needed is to pick the most frequently missed component. Thus, for the generalization of the components in the top-level rules in a model, we can suggest decreasing the number of majors or minors, and the removal of the requirement and exclusion components. This summarizes how we obtained most of the generalization heuristics described in Chapter 4.

For specialization, we had two factors to consider. First, there can be more than one incorrect conclusion reached in a misdiagnosed case, and therefore, we needed a means of determining specific rules to specialize. We chose to split these conclusions into *primary* and *secondary* classes in order to determine how badly a case was misdiagnosed by the model. We defined a closeness measure in Chapter 3 that assigns (to the incorrectly applied rules in these classes) an interpretation of how close a misdiagnosed case would be to correction if these rules were forced to be not satisfied. This measure led to the summed statistics about rules for primary and secondary specializations that could be easily compared with the statistics about candidate rules for generalization.

A second point about specializing a rule concerns how it should be strengthened. This is more difficult than it is for generalization. The reason is that performance information alone indicates only that a rule has been satisfied (and does not indicate which component in a rule should be strengthened or how to add a component to a rule.) The notion of *ease of change* is introduced to help in this problem. The idea is that the components in a rule may be ordered based on an understanding of the nature of the component--that minors are easier to change than majors, and majors are easier to change (preferred over) requirements, etc. Accordingly, a separate heuristic rule was formulated for selecting a component to strengthen in a rule cited for specialization.

This covers most of the heuristics that deal with the top-level rules in the model. We introduced refinement heuristics to get experiments about the intermediate rules which underlie the components in a top-level rule. A model's rules are organized hierarchically and contribute to the higher level rules in a direct way--for example, a requirement component which is not satisfied can be traced back through the rules which may be used to reach this conclusion. Because of this, the introduction of the refinement heuristics provided a way to deal with an important consideration, i.e., how to present the experiments to the human expert? There are many ways to change the model, and we want to give advice in a *systematic* manner. A benefit of using refinement heuristics is that the expert may gauge the level of detail for investigating experiments.

It should be noted that many of the generalization heuristics may be collapsed to a single heuristic rule that suggests the removal of the most frequently missed component without regard to a specific type of component. We have left them separate for the possibility of augmenting them with some background or domain-specific knowledge.

6.1.3.2 Adequacy of the Heuristics

The adequacy of the heuristics can be assessed in two ways: the advice they provide (i.e, the adequacy for covering the kinds of refinements that may be needed to the tabular model,) and the manner in which the advice is presented (i.e., the interaction with the expert and the empirical evidence presented.)

Total coverage of the kinds of refinements is provided by the heuristics, i.e., the heuristics suggest experiments about each of the terms that appear in the tabular model structure. There are refinement heuristics that operate on the requirement and exclusion components in order to obtain more specific experiments than citing the top-level components alone. There are no refinement heuristics for the experiments to decrease or increase the numbers of majors and minors in a rule. Nonetheless, the kinds of refinements (including the change of a rule's confidence level) are limited to changing the existing rules in the model.

Although the system does not suggest to add a new rule, such a capability is secondary to a basic task of refining the rules placed in the model by the expert. Our heuristics refine the rules that the expert thinks are best, and any extensions to the model would be done as a result of experimenting with the existing rules.

146

What is the manner in which the advice is presented? An interactive scheme is used for presenting advice that provides a controlled framework for revision of the rules. The heuristics are domain-independent[11] and are applied on the rules for one diagnosis, which the expert selects. The expert is therefore expected to narrow the experiments suggested by the heuristics to those most consistent with his domain knowledge. Finally, the narrative explanation of the heuristics facilitates the expert's analysis of the empirical evidence that supports the experiments.

The heuristics are built into the system by hand. There is no facility to change them directly by the user. Manipulating the heuristics occurs at the data structure level. The clauses in the heuristic rules have particular (numeric) labels to reference functions, relational operators, and values. Each heuristic is represented by a pair of data structures (one for the left-hand side of the heuristic and the other for the heuristic's right-hand side). Changing a clause involves setting the functional references by using numeric labels, setting the relational operator and any associated values. A set of pointers are used to reference the heuristics. Thus, to change a heuristic rule requires that the appropriate set of pointers are updated after the heuristic's clauses are changed. This is a tedious and very primitive process for which specific improvements have been ignored in the development of SEEK.

Suggestions about language facilities for expressing the heuristics are presented in section 6.2. A language facility offers the possibility for the expert to incorporate domain-specific information into the heuristics to narrow the generation of experiments relevant to the domain.

6.1.4 Dual Sources of Knowledge

SEEK requires that the expert's decision-making knowledge be expressed in the tabular model and that test cases are provided with the correct conclusions. We have made two working assumptions about these dual sources of knowledge. For the tabular model, we have assumed that the model is generally correct--that the model has been thoughtfully prepared although its criteria may require fine-tuning. The expert is expected to know what he's formulating in the model and also to have done his best at preparing

---

[11]The specific parameter values in the current set of heuristics have an intuitive rationale (e.g., the refinement heuristic for adding an item to a requirement component shown in section 4.4.2 uses a specific parameter value to test for inconsistency.) These values may be altered with other information from the domain of application.

it. In this respect, we have focused on suggesting slight changes in generalizing or specializing the model's rules.

In dealing with the cases, one can rarely assume that very large sets are presented with complete accuracy. Nevertheless, we do assume that care is taken in the determination and actual assignment of the expert's correct diagnosis for each of the stored cases. This is critical to SEEK's performance evaluation since rule refinements are derived from case analysis, which compares the model's conclusion with the stored expert's conclusion.

Another point concerns the representativeness of the cases for each conclusion. Informally stated, SEEK works best when there are a large number of test cases, but; how many cases actually should be used for each conclusion? Furthermore, how many cases should be classic examples, and how many should be more difficult cases for differential diagnosis? In this work, we have only assumed that the expert has access to cases which are representative, at least, of those seen in a real-world setting.

To get more information about the nature of cases, the expert may be able to provide not only the correct diagnosis for each case but also the confidence in the diagnosis. This has not been done here; however, further work is needed in order to test whether a better basis for collecting *representative* cases is provided if confidence levels as well as diagnosis can be reliably obtained for each case.

Within the current scheme of requiring that the correct diagnosis for each test case be specified, histograms which display the distribution of cases according to the model's confidence (Chapter 5 presented examples of histograms) are helpful to gain insight into the nature of the cases. When the expert has sufficient credibility in the model's rules, the histograms could be used as indicators for selecting test cases.

6.2 Future Work

In this section, some suggestions for future work are presented. We will consider extensions of specific features in SEEK beginning with the preconditions of model evaluation. Other ideas are suggested for improving the evaluation of the model, the evaluation of the heuristic rules, and for improving the model design process by empirical testing.

148

6.2.1 Treatment of Ties for Model Evaluation

The current implementation allows the expert to select how ties are to be scored. Unfortunately, this is an all-or-nothing option. The problem is that while some conclusions may be considered mutually exclusive and ties are therefore not acceptable, overlap for other diagnoses can occur. Further, the confidence at which ties are acceptable may differ. For unrelated diagnoses, the tied confidence of *definite* may be appropriate. The point is that an improvement over the current scheme for setting ties should be considered--for example, to give the expert the option of selecting the confidence levels at which ties are acceptable and to further specify the diagnostic overlaps which are acceptable at the particular levels.

6.2.2 Cases with multiple conclusions

The cases presented to the program are expected to have a single best diagnosis although there may be several expert's diagnoses stored with a given case. An alternative is to give the expert the option of spliting the diagnoses into two groups: the primary, or top-ranked answer(s) for the case, and the secondary, consisting of all other diagnoses he thinks are reasonable for the model to conclude. With this extension, a case can be scored by means of using the *turnoff* option (currently a global condition for model evaluation) to ignore rules for the secondary diagnoses. Thus, a case with diagnoses such as rheumatoid arthritis as a primary diagnosis and Sjogren's syndrome the secondary diagnosis can be effectively scored by ignoring the secondary conclusion which could be reached at the definite confidence level, and compare the model's top-ranked result with its confidence in rheumatoid arthritis.

6.2.3 Gathering statistics

If we look at the steps involved in identifying a candidate rule for generalization, the method used to compute the closeness measure deserves attention. The rule tracing procedure maintains two counts on the number of components satisfied and the number of components needed for satisfaction. These counts are used to compute a rule's percentage of total satisfaction.

Whether an individual component in a rule is totally satisfied is not taken into consideration in arriving at the percentage measure. For all the top-level rules, each consisting of numbers of majors and minors, a requirement and an exclusion, additional weighting may be given to some components, for example, based on being totally satisfied

149

components. This may produce a better measure, however, of the partially satisfied rules to select a candidate rule to generalize.

The rule with maximum percentage of satisfaction and with minimal confidence needed to correct the case is selected as a candidate rule for generalization. In this rule, the first unsatisfied component found is identified for removal. The rule may have other unsatisfied components, which are ignored by our scheme. An extension to this is to identify all unsatisfied components. As an example, consider rule R in Figure 6-2 which is a candidate rule for generalization. Suppose rule R has 3 cases supporting its generalization, and the first unsatisfied component for each of these three cases is A, A, and B. Thus, component A would be chosen for removal since it is the most frequently missed component among the three cases according to this criterion. But for cases 1 and 2, component B is also unsatisfied.

```
Rule R:    A & B & C -> DX1

CASE 1:    U    U    S
CASE 2:    U    U    S
CASE 3:    S    U    S

U:   unsatisfied component
S:   satisfied component
```

Figure 6-2:   Rule with Unsatisfied Components

Thus if the method first gathers all unsatisfied components and assigns them to the cases individually there could be a more informed pattern to be extracted as shown in this example. Along the same line a rule's components may be ordered explicitly according to preference in changing the components. This may be particularly useful for rules that reach intermediate conclusions.[12]

In gathering the statistics about specialization, two kinds of conclusions are noted: primary--refers to the model's highest ranked incorrect conclusion in a case, and secondary--refers to all other incorrect conclusions reached in a case. The closeness measure for the rule responsible for the primary conclusion is an interpretation about how close the case would be to correction if the rule were forced to be not satisfied. This measure is derived from the number of rules incorrectly satisfied and the number of incorrect conclusions reached in a misdiagnosed case.

---

[12]We note that the top-level rules have a fixed ordering of components (majors, minors, requirement, and exclusion), from which it seemed more systematic and reasonable that the first unsatisfied component found in the rule be used.

150

As an example from the methods described in section 3.3, the interpretation of *1 rule for the primary conclusion and more than 1 incorrect conclusions* says that if the rule is forced to be not satisfied, the case would *have a better chance for correction*. This can be misleading since we don't take into account the actual number of incorrect conclusions that were reached. Obviously, one could try to use this information by extending the current set of interpretations for specialization experiments. For example, the number of incorrect conclusions reached in a case could give a better picture of how badly the model actually performed on a case. This could be used to indicate interpretations such as *will remove the top-ranked incorrect conclusion for the case and will be closer to being correct but a few problems still remain* if the number of other incorrect conclusions were less than a small yet prespecified threshold value. Another one could be *will remove the top-ranked incorrect conclusion but forget about correcting the case by specializations since there are many other problems* if many incorrect conclusions were reached in the case.

Although some extensions can be made and new statistics proposed, the more difficult task is to determine how the statistics are to be put to use in the heuristics. We believe that continued experience with the program on different models and careful monitoring of the experiments suggested and those that were not, may lead to finding statistics which are useful. There are two features in SEEK which can help--a trace of the execution of the heuristics, and the notification that an experiment could not be suggested when all heuristics fail for a particular rule.

6.2.4 Model Execution Improvements

The model is evaluated by invoking all rules on each case in the data base. The execution time for this task varies according to the number of rules in the model and the total number of cases. In Figure, 6-3, the dimensions and execution times for three models are shown. Because of the exhaustive evaluation of the model for all cases, improvements in efficiency can come from organizing the model with possibly fewer rules and a selective evaluation of the tables. The first extension might be accomplished by replacing the rules which determine the numbers of majors and minors with a special functional argument in a rule.

An abstract example of the current method of computing the numbers of majors and minors is shown next. It is a means of computing the number of majors taken from that rule with the most number of items satisfied in its left-hand side, and it is derived from

MODELS

	M1	M2	M3
Number of cases:	143	199	146
Number of rules:	794	981	169
Total number of components in the rules:	4195	4207	841
Time (CPU seconds) on DEC 2060T:	49	68	16

Figure 6-3: Performance in Evaluation of 3 Models

our implementation to be consistent with the EXPERT syntax. However, a more concise form would be a single rule shown below these 3 rules with a function COUNT that returns a value. This would require changes to the control strategy to, in effect, evaluate this rule differently, and to assign the value to the right-hand side of the rule.

[1: a, b, c] -> 1 Major for DX1
[2: a, b, c] -> 2 Majors ”   ”
[3: a, b, c] -> 3 Majors ”   ”

[COUNT: a, b, c] -> MJ, value

The second improvement concerns the evaluation of the tables. In EXPERT syntax, rules can be organized into groups called HH tables with the following syntax: IF condition THEN evaluate collection of rules. The IF part contains conditions to be satisfied prior to considering the rules in the THEN part. If there exists a preprocess for computing valid conditions under which a table should be evaluated, then some efficiency could be gained.

6.2.5 Evaluation of the Heuristic Rules

The heuristics are evaluated after being filled in with the required statistics. For a given rule in the model, most of the heuristics are evaluated. Some other heuristics are not tried because they are triggered only for the refinement of previously suggested experiments. These refinement heuristics go deeper in the analysis of rules and are invoked only on demand by the model designer. The evaluation of the heuristics consists of a single cycle[13] of testing the conditions and posting the experiments on a list of suggested rule refinements for the model designer to consider.

---

[13]with the exception of the heuristic rules for adding an item to a component (e.g., the refinement heuristic for strengthening a requirement component, described in section 4.4.2 is evaluated at least once and as many times as the number of items appearing in a list of items (majors) that are used to select an item;)

A single cycle follows from the assumption that the heuristics contain enough information to suggest the most obvious changes. For example, the function MFMC, which determines the *most frequently missed component* among the cases supporting the generalization of a rule, has been found to be quite adequate. However, an extension of this scheme that would draw out more experimental changes can be based on multiple cycles of heuristic evaluation. For example, when several cases support the generalization of a rule R, and the MFMC function is used to pick a component for deletion as in:

```
Cases supporting the
generalization of R:    1   3   5   6   7  15  17

Missing  component:     A   A   B   C   A   C   C
```

Here, seven cases support the generalization of rule R and the MFMC is really a tie between two components A and C. In practice, MFMC returns A and the remaining cases would go unnoticed, even though the support for removing C occurs in equal numbers as that for removing A.

However, if we remove those cases that were accounted for in the first evaluation cycle, and start a second evaluation of the heuristics, then the cases supporting C in this example would be given a chance of suggesting experiments. The point is that multiple evaluations of the heuristics could be tried in situations like the generalization heuristics that use the MFMC function. When there are few cases supporting the generalization of the rules, a single pass should suffice.

6.2.6 Adding Background Information to the Heuristics

One of the main advantages of the heuristics is that they are domain independent.[14] So long as the expert's knowledge is expressed in the tabular model format, it makes no difference whether the model is for rheumatology, dermatology, or auto-repair. Also, the heuristics operate in exactly the same way for each of the tables of rules.

There is no domain-specific component in the heuristics. The expert uses his experience when reviewing and choosing the experiments suggested by the heuristics, without which it would be difficult to engage in sessions of model refinement. If we were to extend the capabilities of SEEK, the most difficult aspect would be to guide the expert

---

[14]In the current implementation, the heuristics require only background information of orderings that are part of general medical conventions, and not specifically related to a particular domain.

in making appropriate changes in discriminating between the conclusions and in helping incorporate the knowledge which is needed to make medically sound refinements.

In our experiments with SEEK, we have sometimes been told that the system makes reasonable suggestions for the cases at hand, which nevertheless are not as medically sound as alternatives might be. The former of course is to be expected, since the advice is derived from case review, but the point is that the advice is meant to force the expert to rethink his criteria in light of these phenomena. The program is supposed to help the expert test his rules and suggest ways to change them, but it is not designed to carry out the task of getting a medically consistent set of rules on its own. Since experiential knowledge for the expert is largely a matter of empirical association, much of the medical soundness consists of missing empirical knowledge that the expert is able to reconsider. For instance, specific correlations of findings may be brought to the expert's attention as a result of seeing the performance of the rules, which SEEK is intended to assist in drawing out. The expert knows how to interpret the experiments and decides which experiments to pursue.

Thus, the knowledge about how and why a certain change should be tried or preferred over another is largely based on rethinking the model, so as to uncover what is lacking in it. For example, the rethinking process may determine that a pair of findings may occur together, though unexpectedly, and possibly what is needed to improve the model is that one of the findings should be expanded into its constituent observations to correctly discriminate between competing diagnoses.

However, what is the possibility of introducing some domain expertise into the heuristics to make the program ignore certain changes and go on to others? An example from the rheumatology domain may clarify the problem. For the diseases known as mixed connective tissue diseases, the laboratory finding of RNP is a highly specific indication of the disease and is incorporated as a requirement in the table for MCTD.

Now consider what the program does in a situation where an experiment has been generated to delete the requirement component of an MCTD rule containing a conjunction of the finding RNP and other findings. The program can refine the experiment and look for a particular finding to be removed at the request of the expert. Since it is only checking for what is satisfied and not satisfied, the program reports back the best item to

154

change on this basis alone. If the cases are accurate and *complete*, the experiment is probably empirically sound. But the expert may believe that the rule should contain always the finding of RNP and never be considered for removal. The heuristic might be augmented with knowledge that says if the experiment is to delete a requirement component of an MCTD rule, then do not suggest the removal of the finding RNP because he says so and therefore pick something else in the rule.

Another example where background information is important is in adding a component to a rule. Our solution is to let the expert tell the program which list of criteria of majors or minors should be used to select a component to change (an example of this was shown in Chapter 4). Default preferences used by the heuristics are based on the rule's confidence--if the confidence is *definite* or *probable* then use the major list; if the confidence is *possible* then use the minor list. It may be advantageous to have this information incorporated in the heuristics directly by the expert. Another example is derived from our experience with a threshold setting to compare with a rule's percentage of the time it was significant when invoked. After some experiments with a specific rheumatology model and its associated cases, we arrived at a threshold setting of 40%. The heuristic incorporating the expression was to determine a specialization experiment for decreasing a rule's confidence. The expression was: "a rule's rate of significance must be less than 40%," which was used to determine how many cases were allowed to be lost.

These are a few examples that point out the kind of background information which might improve upon the generation of rule refinement experiments. How should this background information be acquired from the expert? We see three modes. One is in the context of a session where the expert is prompted with questions after an experiment is accepted. The information may then be accessible to the heuristics, such as for an experiment which deletes the requirement component in an MCTD rule. Another mode is to have a distinct set of heuristics for each tabular model defining a disease. The advantage of this approach is that the heuristics might then be tailored to the specific diseases. The third mode could combine the first two. Thus, the heuristics for each disease may be initially set up as they exist currently, then they are augmented with some constraints about which components to ignore for possible experiments, while the results of subsequent experimental trials would be used by the expert to refine the heuristics.

The first step, however, is to have a convenient means for the expression of the heuristics by the expert. Although our heuristics currently can be viewed by the user, they are represented and manipulated within FORTRAN arrays and consequently only those familiar with the program can modify them. For the user, there is a translator which produces a readable version of the heuristics but there is no facility available to change them directly.

A language for expressing the heuristics is needed. We envision a language of functional expressions with a simple Algol-like syntax in which the expert may express certain parameter values or preferences in changing the rules. An example can be taken from the the heuristic rule to suggest the decrease of the number of majors in a rule:

If   NGEN(R) > NSPEC(R)

       & MFMC(R) = "majors"

Then DECREASE MAJORS(R).

The functional labels specify the statistical values to be compared, for example, NGEN indicates the number of cases supporting the generalization of a rule. The THEN part indicates the rule refinements such as DECREASE. The idea we have about this language is similar to the language for expressing domain-specific rules in selecting laboratory techniques in the design of genetic experiments in MOLGEN [10] [40], where the rules are associated with specific laboratory techniques represented in the MOLGEN knowledge base [39].

The kinds of functions for specifying background information in our heuristics may be simple predicates that express particular components or rules to be ignored in generating experiments. Another function could be used to set the list of criteria to be used for selecting a component to add to a rule. In our example for RNP, a function which is referenced in the heuristics for changing the MCTD rules might be specified by *NOT(RNP)* to indicate that the component should be ignored in generating experiments. Furthermore, exceptions of this kind may be explained by the expert's reasons for specifying them. Associating a line of English text would do this.

In general, having a convenient way for expressing this kind of background information should prove helpful to tailor and augment the heuristics by the expert. In this way, we may get a better understanding of the decision-making involved in selecting experiments.

156

6.2.7 Automatic Search for Experiments

In this section, we propose a means of extending the generation of experiments by having the system suggest and carry out multiple experiments. First, let's review the current method of generating experiments.

Our method for generating experiments requires the expert's involvement. First, he must focus on a conclusion (rules for a particular tabular model) and subsequently request experiments about these rules. Secondly, the expert must select an experiment to try. These two action requirements are a systematic and simple means of forcing the expert to think about his rules. Once this is done, SEEK takes over and the process of generating experiments (i.e., gathering performance statistics, evaluating the heuristics) is carried out. If the expert has focused on a conclusion DX1, and requests experiments for DX1, SEEK's analysis is split into two groups according to conclusion DX1 and all others conclusions.

All experiments for the rules that conclude DX1 are ranked according to a simple criterion that uses the following statistical values about each rule: the number of cases suggesting the generalization of the rule and the number of cases suggesting the specialization of the rule. The best experiment in terms of performance improvement is the first one presented (e.g., the experiment for rule x in Figure 6-4). This is the current method of interaction necessary for generating experiments.

```
refinement to rule x concluding DX1
  .
  .
  .
refinement to rule z concluding DX1
```

Figure 6-4:   List of Rule Refinement Experiments

The experiments suggested are presented with respect to the rules for one conclusion and against all cases. An extension to this scheme is to reduce the expert's involvement by an automatic search scheme. The idea is to provide a more global analysis than that provided by the single view of one conclusion versus all others.

From the expert's standpoint, our extension would require only that he request experiments rather than additionally citing a particular conclusion. The extension consists of two parts. The first is to look at the current performance and to generate experiments for all conclusions, and to report either the best single experiment to try over *all*

conclusions, or the best experiment for each one of the conclusions. Thus, for DX1, ...,
DXN the program first would generate the experiments for these conclusions and then it
reports back the single best one overall, possibly including some others that are close in
potential performance improvement. This is simply a best-first search that is based on the
current performance of the model.

The second part uses the results of this search by actually executing the single best-
ranked experiment and possibly continuing to some predefined depth. The results of this
cycle of *generate experiments -- and execute the best one* could be reported in the
Before/After summary form along with the experiment (and explanation). To assess
whether an experiment produces positive results, a simple criterion is to check if there is a
gain in correcting the cases -- that the true positives increase from one experiment to the
next. Thus, the success of any particular experiment may be based on the comparison of
the "bottom-line" results provided in the Before/After summary.

For example, the use of a simple comparison of the numbers of true positives from
before and after an experiment, would signal negative results when the true positives
decrease. The experiment that caused the negative results or any of the earlier (positive)
experiments should be brought to the expert's attention. The expert can possibly be given
the option of stepping through each of the experiments or to select the one that caused the
problem. In the stepping mode, if the expert doesn't agree with some experiment taken
(even though it resulted in performance improvement) he may stop the process and
investigate the rules and criteria which comprise them. As an example, Figure 6-5 shows a
hypothetical trace of the experiments tried along with the explanations and summary of
performance.

Finally, in the current implementation, a trace of the experiments tried and those
that were accepted is maintained for analysis after a session is terminated. Finding ways
of using this information during the course of a model refinement session should be
considered in line with the search scheme suggested above.

6.2.8 Adding New Knowledge to the Model

The methods described in the thesis have concentrated on the revision of existing
rules in the model by removing or decreasing components, and adding or increasing
components. Nonetheless, we stated in Chapter 1 that a small model in rheumatology was

Experiment 1
>   Delete the requirement component in rule 89.
>   (explanation)
>   Results
>   Before   After
>   .
>   .
>   .

Experiment 2
>   Decrease the number of majors in rule 90. Value changed: 3 to 2.
>   (explanation)
>   Results
>   Before   After
>   .
>   .
>   .

Figure 6-5:   Trace of Search Scheme - Multiple Experiments

initially developed, and that after many cycles of testing and revision the model was expanded to the point of containing several times the number of findings, rules and conclusions. In this section, we consider this issue of adding knowledge to the model, i.e., to incorporate new elements, as a result of empirical testing. These might include inserting, combining, or deleting the majors and minor findings, and abstracting intermediate hypotheses.

One can obviously expand the model directly without knowledge of the current performance of the model. In this case, the expert introduces new diseases in the form of ables, with corresponding new findings and intermediate results added to cover the broader domain area. We usually expect the expert to start with a limited size model; and to reach a realistic performing model, he typically has to expand the knowledge base, with some of the findings being decomposed into more refined descriptions, new intermediate conclusions introduced to group the findings, etc.

But what is involved in drawing out and adding new knowledge to a model as a result of empirical testing? We want to ease the analysis process in determining a model xtension that may be tried. Extensions can be the introduction of more detailed findings o replace an existing finding, the grouping of several findings into a rule that reaches a ew intermediate result, or the spliting of a rule into more than one rule for reaching a articular result. The reasoning involved in determining an appropriate extension of the model can be a complex problem that may be appreciated by looking at an example. The key idea is that none of the experiments tried seems to get good results. The following example focuses on the analysis of one of the experiments.

Suppose that a rule x for *possible* MCTD requires 3 majors to fire the rule, and a generalization experiment tried on this rule was the decrease of the number of majors to 2. Suppose the experiment resulted in several cases that were misdiagnosed by this rule.

The first step in analyzing the results is to cite the counterexamples of the rule refinement experiment to make sure they appear to be accurately described, with the rule cited so that the case data that satisfied the rule's conditions are shown. From this, one can possibly determine changes to the criteria--replacing an item in the major component with either more specific findings (e.g., replacing an item call *pulmonary disease* with more specific items such as *pleuritis* and *CO diffusing capacity < 40%*), or replacing several items with a more general item.[15]

In our example with rule x, the expert would have to rationalize the conditions in the rule containing 2 majors by analyzing the cases. Assuming that the case data are accurate, the expert must do two things. First, he must check that 2 majors makes sense to confirm the diagnosis of *possible* MCTD, and secondly, he must see if they are sufficiently specific to discriminate between MCTD and the stored answers in the cases misdiagnosed by the rule.

It is through this analysis that the expert must determine how to change, for example, the majors for MCTD. Given that the rule is medically sound for confirming the diagnosis of MCTD, the analysis is focused on the rule's discrimination with other diseases. Starting with the expected conclusions in the cases misdiagnosed by the rule, suppose there is a high frequency of one diagnosis among these cases (e.g. most of the cases misdiagnosed by rule x have the expected conclusion of SLE). A simple means of assessing the major is by looking at their frequency in the cases with the conclusion of SLE. Suppose the majors for MCTD are listed and one item -- *pulmonary disease* -- had high frequency in the SLE cases. So what does this mean?

---

[15]Although the expert can split a rule or combine others into a rule, the system does not actually generate the advice to say, for example, "split the component labeled *pulmonary disease* into *a* and *b* and replace *pulmonary disease* in the majors for MCTD with these items".

160

An item labeled *pulmonary disease* appears in the major criteria for the disease MCTD. Since the expert previously identified the item as a major, we may assume this item is rationally compatible for this disease. But the empirical results reveal that this item is not specific to MCTD alone. A possible solution is that the major of *pulmonary disease* item may be refined by replacing it with other items to discriminate the MCTD cases from the SLE cases.[16] The expert is the only one to do this even if there exists a rule for pulmonary disease. He analyzes the results to uncover the existence of a potential conflict in the use of a particular item. In this context, SEEK provides a fundamental tool to discover details within the data that can help the expert's determination of how, for example, *pulmonary disease* can be refined.

However, the guidance for the analysis of negative (unfavorable) performance results of an experiment is limited to suggestions of the tools to be used as opposed to actually carrying out (parts of) this analysis automatically. The latter may be tried by combining the application of the tools into a procedure which would be invoked based on the recognition of an experiment's poor results. We can speculate that a heuristic rule which looks for negative results of certain kinds of generalization experiments would have as its right-hand side a procedure which would, in effect, summarize details of the experiment's impact. The benefits of this would be at least to improve the efficiency of the analysis of the experimental results. However, this is just a first step in getting a better understanding of a very difficult issue.[17]

---

[16] The expert may not be able to uncover something that will resolve the problem, i.e., the single item found can not be refined. In this case, the item previously believed to be important in reaching the diagnosis of MCTD, may be removed from the majors for MCTD, or possibly added to the exclusions for the SLE criteria.

[17] Since the writing of my dissertation, certain research has been done at Rutgers which follows through on many of the ideas mentioned in this section 6.2. This work has been carried out by Allen Ginsberg, Sholom Weiss, and myself and has resulted in a new system called **SEEK2** [16]. Specifically, there are three key ideas in **SEEK2** that represent concrete implementations of the ideas that I mentioned: (a) **SEEK2** does knowledge base refinement for a more general class of knowledge bases than SEEK, i.e., restrictions to tabular model format have been removed; (b) **SEEK2** has an "automatic pilot" capability, i.e., it can automatically generate and incorporate a sequence of plausible refinements that **SEEK2** itself has verifed to lead to a significant improvement in knowledge base performance; (c) a metalanguage for knowledge base refinement has been specified which allows both domain-independent and domain-specific metaknowledge to be formally expressed and used in the refinement process.

6.3 Conclusion

The scheme presented in this thesis has been tested in rheumatology. Another application that was tried independently was in dermatology [43]. These are two real-world applications to assess our empirical analysis approach. The goal of this thesis has been to show that performance information can be usefully employed in the design of large real-world expert models. A major result is that a unified framework for expert model design and testing can be built that facilitates the experimentation with expert knowledge. Our specific experimental results have shown that SEEK provides the tools to build and efficiently maintain a high performance rheumatology model[18] which consists of 900 findings, 600 intermediate conclusions, and over 1000 production rules for nearly 30 rheumatic diseases. Furthermore, while the dimensions of the dermatology model are similar to those in the rheumatology model, it is important to note that this model was developed in a relatively short amount of time.[19]

The significance of SEEK's scheme of empirical testing is its ability to put empirical results to use for the generation of intelligent advice about rule refinement. Although the advice suggests ways of improving model performance on a data base of test cases, the importance of advice is to stimulate the expert's rethinking of his domain--to provoke further investigation of his decision making knowledge in the form of a tabular model-- based on the explicit results of empirical analysis. We believe that the integration of the methods described in this thesis provides the controlled framework to carry out the empirical inquiry necessary to build high performance diagnostic consultation systems.

The successful development of the SEEK program has shown that the complexity of the model building task can be manageably handled by providing a systematic means for acquiring decision-making knowledge, which also helps in testing this knowledge within a single framework. The effectiveness of SEEK in offering advice about rule refinement centers on a relatively accurate description of the expert's criteria in the form of tables. This has been proven in rheumatology and SEEK's advice based on case experience can improve performance as was demonstrated in the sample session in chapter 5.

---

[18] at a rate of more than 90% correct diagnosis on 150 cases

[19] less than 1 man year's effort.

162

A relatively simple representation that is suitable for capturing the expert's knowledge is important. The expert understands how his knowledge is used within the representation, and the system produces meaningful results in the form of advice about revising it.

Finding a sufficiently expressive knowledge representation has been one of the main concerns in the application of AI techniques and is driven by the needs of the application area. This is particularly true for the work presented in this thesis. Much of the insight into what would be a useful assistant came from our practical experience with rheumatology problems. Since the tabular model is a format that is familiar to physicians and also one that is directly representable in the machine, an effective line of communication is opened. The point is that much stands to be gained in the design of an effective assistance program by working closely within a real application area.

We have identified explicit points in the model design and empirical testing framework where various kinds of interaction with the expert control and focus experimentation with his knowledge. An important area for the design of future SEEK-like systems is to find language facilities for meaningful interactive model building and testing. We believe that the foundation for this has been developed with the heuristics and command facilities in the SEEK program, and we have suggested that the development of a language facility for the expression and customization of heuristic rules is a first step in gaining a better understanding of the process of empirical experimentation. Finally, the methods described in this thesis should be applied to other domains. With these experiences, new ideas and extensions may be found that might further our understanding of capturing expert knowledge in a computer.

I. Command Facilities

This appendix provides a description of the commands available to the user of SEEK. The user has the option of using these commands directly or to let the system prompt him in the form of menus, which are used in the sample session in Chapter 5.

EDIT

- Enters a structured editor to edit a tabular model. A tabular model is organized by final diagnoses and includes slots for major and minor observations, diagnostic rules for confidence levels: definite, probable, possible, and rules for intermediate conclusions which are used by the diagnostic rules. Once in the editor, help facilities are available by typing ESC-H (escape H), ESC-E, or ESC-S.

- Syntax: EDIT [MODELNAME]

CASES

- Enter the EXPERT consultation system to enter or to revise cases. Once in EXPERT, help facilities are available by typing "?".

- Syntax: CASES

TEST

- To load a model for performance analysis by SEEK. Useful commands to issue immediately after loading a model are: TIES, TUrnoff. The TEST command must be issued prior to any analysis commands: SUM, ANalyze, ADvise, EXPeriments.

- Syntax: TEST

TIES

- Typing TIES allows the designer to specify a condition for performance evaluation: to determine treatment of ties in confidence for the expert's conclusion and the model's different conclusion in each of the cases.

- Syntax: TIES

TUrnoff

- To ignore the analysis of rules and cases for a specified final diagnosis.

- Syntax: TUrnoff

SUM

- To obtain a performance summary of the model on the cases. Results are organized by final diagnoses. The SUM command must be issued once a "dynamic" version of the model is created (see WHATIF), or immediately after a predecessor version is restored (see BACK). A switch "/S" on the SUM command will produce a list of cases with the values for the expert's stored conclusion and the model's conclusion assigned to each case.

- Syntax: SUM[/S]

DCASE

- To obtain a histogram display of the distribution of case performance for a specified final diagnosis. If no final diagnosis is specified then all final diagnoses are shown for which there exists cases with matching stored expert conclusions. MNE is mnemonic for final diagnosis.

- Syntax: DCASE [(MNE)]

SCore

- To list the model's conclusions for a specified case number. All cases are listed if no argument is specified.

- Syntax: SCore [(CASE#)]

HITs

- To display the performance of a rule on the stored cases. Argument is a rule number.

- Syntax: HITs(rule#)

2SUM

- To show the summary of performance (see SUM) as a result of making an experimental change to the model, in a "before" and "after" format. This command is valid only when a model refinement experiment (see WHATIF) is not accepted by the designer and prior to making any subsequent changes to the model. It is useful because it saves the results of the most recent experiment and thus does not require the re-execution of the experiment on the cases.

- Syntax: 2SUM

EFFECT

- To show the results of making an experimental change to the model on each case. This command is used in conjunction with the 2SUM command. Results include the disposition of each case for a specified diagnosis.

- Syntax: EFFECT [(MNE)]

ANalyze

- To enter analysis mode. The program prompts the designer for a basis of analysis: "single case" or "all cases". In "single case", a specified case is retrieved. In "all cases", rules for a specified final diagnosis are subjected to analysis over all stored cases.

- Syntax: ANalysis

VIEW

- This command is used in the "all cases" basis of analysis (see ANalysis). It shows two numbers for each rule - indicating that the rule is a potential candidate for generalization or specialization in the respective number of cases. If there are x cases for generalization: if the rule is satisfied, then x misdiagnosed cases would be correctly diagnosed. If there are y cases for specialization: if the rule is not satisfied, then y misdiagnosed cases would have improved chances of being correctly diagnosed.

- Syntax: VIEW

GEN

- This command shows information about the cases supporting the generalization of each rule (see VIEW). It shows the number of major and minor observations satisfied (for the expert's diagnosis) in the case; the model's incorrect conclusion; and, the first unsatisfied component in the rule.

- Either zero or two arguments can be specified:

      ARG1 - rule number
      ARG2 - "CASE", "DX", or "ALL"

- If no arguments are specified, all rules are listed (ARG1) with all the information available (ARG2 - "ALL").

- Syntax: GEN [(ARG1,ARG2)]

SPEC

- SPEC shows information about the cases supporting the specialization of each rule (see VIEW). It shows the number of major and minor observations satisfied (for the expert's diagnosis) in the case, and the expert's (correct) conclusion.

- Either zero or two arguments can be specified:

    ARG1 - rule number
    ARG2 - "CASE" or "ALL"

- If no arguments are specified, all rules are listed (ARG1) with all the information available (ARG2 - "ALL").

- Syntax: SPEC [(ARG1,ARG2)]

EXPeriments

- Produces a list of suggested changes to be made to the rules for a specified diagnosis. The experiments are ordered by maximum potential gain in performance on the cases.

- Syntax: EXPeriments(MNE)

ADvise

- Produces a list of suggested changes (see EXPeriments) to the model and a statement to explain why a change is suggested.

- Syntax: ADvise(MNE)

REFINements

- To produce a list of refined changes for a specified experiment (see EXPeriments). One argument is required to specify the number of the experiment for which refinements are sought.

- Syntax: REFINements(EXPnumber)

WHY

- To produce an explanation of a suggested change to the model. One argument is required to specify the number of the experiment.

- Syntax: WHY(EXPnumber)

PRECedence

- To produce the list of experiments (see EXPeriments) in order of reasonable changes to be made to the model.

- Syntax: PRECedence(MNE)

ASSESS

- To evaluate an experiment or pair of experiments (see EXPeriments, PRECedence) in terms of potential performance gain and reasonable changes. One or two arguments can be specified:

  ARG1 - experiment number1
  ARG2 - experiment number2

- Syntax: ASSESS(ARG1 [,ARG2])

WHATIF

- The WHATIF command is used to conditionally incorporate in the model one or more experimental modifications to the rules. The result is a summary of performance (see SUM) of the effect of the change on the cases. The output format is based on "before" and "after" the changes are made to the model. The designer is prompted to accept the changes and therefore to form a new version of the model, or to reject the changes.

- Note that changes made by WHATIF are dynamic and are in effect for the duration of the current session in SEEK. See the BACK command to restore the model to a previous version of the model as a result of an accepted WHATIF. An accepted WHATIF can be permanently incorporated into the model by issuing the SAVE command.

- Syntax: WHATIF(FIXES) where FIXES are:

    FIX1 && FIX2 && ... && FIXn   (n<=8)

- Each FIX is of the form:

            TYPE([ATTRIBUTE,] OBJECT, VALUE)
            where
            if TYPE is "Generalize" or "Specialize"
            then   ATTRIBUTE is mnemonic label of a rule's component
                      OBJECT is rule number
                      VALUE is a number (n>0) or "D" (delete component)
            OR
            if TYPE is "ADD"   (to add components to a rule)
               or "INSERT"   (to insert a new rule)
            then   ATTRIBUTE is ignored
                      OBJECT is rule number
                      VALUE is a logical combination of components
            OR
            if TYPE is "MOVe"
            then   ATTRIBUTE is ignored
                      OBJECT is rule number
                      VALUE is "NULL", "POSSible", "PROBable",
                         or "DEFinite"

FORward

- FORward command is the same as WHATIF except that the fix is incorporated into a new version of the model without asking the designer to accept or to reject it.

- Syntax: FORward(FIXES)

BACK

- BACK is used to backup to a previous version (during the current session) of the model. Whenever WHATIF is accepted or FORward is issued, SEEK produces a reference label for the new version of the model. Use the numeric part of the label to backup to a previous version (the default value is zero when TEST mode is entered). Alternatively, a relative negative-valued reference number can be used (e.g., -1 to restore to the most recent previous version of the model). Use VERSion command to obtain the current version number.

- NOTE: To ensure precise performance information, issue SUM command immediately after BACK.

- Syntax: BACK(number)

SAVE

- To save (i.e., to make permanent) the current version of the model as a result of any dynamic changes (see WHATIF, FORward) made during the current session.

- Syntax: SAVE

COMPILE

- To compile the model. One argument is required to specify the model file name.

- Syntax: COMPILE(MODELNAME)

IGNORE

- To ignore the dynamic changes (see WHATIF, FORward) incorporated during the current session and start over.

- Syntax: IGNORE

WHATIS

- To get a description of parts of the model. One argument is required.

- If a numeric argument is specified, it is interpreted as a rule number. The rule matching the rule number is displayed.

- If an alphameric argument is specified, it is interpreted as a mnemonic for a finding or conclusion in the model.

- Syntax: WHATIS(ARG)

VERsion

- The current version number as a result of dynamic changes (see WHATIF, FORward) to the model is displayed.

- Syntax: VERSion

TOP

- To produce a pretty display of the major and minor observations for a specified final diagnosis.

- Syntax: TOP(MNE)

FIND

- To list the findings in the questionnaire section of the model.

- Syntax: FIND

NEW

- To start a new session with SEEK.

- Syntax: NEW

Quit

- To exit SEEK directly.

- Syntax: Quit

2DX

- List the cases with more than one Reviewer's diagnosis.

- Syntax: 2DX

MULTi-dx

- This allows the model designer to determine how cases with more than one Reviewer's diagnosis are to be treated.

- Syntax: MULTi-dx

SEARCH

- To enter the EXPERT Data Base Search Program. This program allows the model designer to get statistical information by specifying search patterns. Help facilities exist once in the SEARCH program.

- Syntax: SEARCH

GFREQ

- To compile frequencies of majors or minors for all conclusion and on over all cases. This produces a file with extension ".FRQ" attached to model filename. To obtain specific frequencies, use the OFREQ command.

- Syntax: GFREQ

OFREQ

- To obtain frequencies of majors or minors on cases with a specified Reviewer's Diagnosis. Two arguments are required: ARG1 - mnemonic of major or minor criteria; ARG2 - mnemonic of a final conclusion or "*" to see freqs of ARG1 over ALL conclusions (Example: OFREQ(MJRA,*) will show freqs about the majors for RA over all conclusions.)

- Syntax: OFREQ(ARG1,ARG2)

SAMPLe-session

- Shows a sample session with SEEK.

- Does not include the use of the EDIT facilities.

II. Tabular Model Format

This appendix shows an example of how a tabular model is encoded into the EXPERT [51] syntax used by SEEK. There are three formats. The first format represents the tabular model which is prepared by the expert. This model is then entered into the system by using SEEK's editor. Editing commands are tailored to the tabular model structure that makes this translation a relatively easy process. The second format is the result of entering the model via SEEK's editor. The third format shows the tabular model in the EXPERT syntax. A translator takes the model in the structured editor's format and produces an EXPERT model file. Finally, EXPERT's compiler program translates the model file into a format (not shown in the appendix) that is executable by the EXPERT consultation program.

II.1 Initial Model Format

Shown below is an example of a model that is prepared by the expert. It shows the major and minor observations for the diagnosis of MCTD as well as the rules for the three confidence levels of *Definite*. *Probable*, and *Possible*. In this example, the expert has prepared one rule at the definite confidence level, two rules at the probable confidence level, and three rules for *possible* MCTD. The rule labeled **A.** at the probable level can be read as: 3 or more majors for MCTD and a conjunctive requirement of the lab results *anti-RNP positive with ENA titer >1:1000*. There is no exclusion indicated for this rule. The rule labeled **B.** at the probable level needs two majors with at least one of them to be taken from the indicated majors of *Raynaud's or esophageal hypomotility, CO diff capacity <70%, or severe Myositis*. Also, two or more minors are needed by this rule as well as the requirement and exclusionary values that are needed by rule **A** for *probable* MCTD.

Proposed Criteria for MCTD
Mixed connective tissue disease

Major Criteria
----
1. Raynaud's or esophageal hypomotility
2. Swollen hands, observed
3. Sclerodactyly
4. CO diff capacity, % nl: <70
5. Myositis, severe

Minor Criteria
----
1. Alopecia
2. WBC count, /cmm: <4000
3. Anemia – <=10 gm% female, <= 12 gm% male
4. Pleuritis
5. Pericarditis
6. Arthritis <=6 wks, or non-polyarticular
7. Malar (butterfly) rash
8. Platelet count, /cmm (thousands): <100
9. Myositis, mild

	Definite	Probable	Possible
CLIN	A. 4 majors	A. 3 majors	A. 3 majors
		B. 2 majors, incl 1 or more from #1, #4, #5 2 minors	B. 2 majors
			C. 1 major 3 minors
REQD	anti-RNP +, with ENA $>=1:4000$	anti-RNP +, with ENA $>=1:1000$	A. No requirements
			B. anti-RNP +, with ENA $>=1:100$
			C. anti-RNP +, with ENA $>=1:100$
EXCL	anti-Sm +	none	none

II.2 SEEK Editor-Format of the Model

This section shows the equivalent model as a result of entering it in the SEEK editor. A partial listing of the editor commands available to encode and update a tabular model is presented below.

```
escape T      EDIT the NAME for the specified diagnosis
              or treatment.
escape M      EDIT the MAJORS.
escape N      EDIT the MINORS.
escape D      EDIT the DEFINITE RULES.
escape R      EDIT the PROBABLE RULES.
escape O      EDIT the POSSIBLE RULES.
escape I      EDIT the INTERMEDIATE RULES.
escape K      DELETE a TABLE for the specified diagnosis
              or treatment.
escape L      LIST a TABLE
control-T     INSERT a TEMPLATE for a new TABLE.
control-R     INSERT a TEMPLATE for a new RULE SET.
escape P      MOVE a TABLE to a different position.
escape W      TYPE a DIRECTORY of the diagnosis and
              treatment tables.
```

Commands for Editing Tables

There are four main sections to the SEEK Editor-Format. The first section contains the English description of the diagnosis of MCTD which is to be used during a consultation session.

The description of the final diagnosis is followed by the lists of majors and minors that form the second section of the model's editor format. Here, each item is identified by a mnemonic label. We summarize below several ways to indicate special treatment of an item for which a switch (indicated by the symbol "/") may be appended to its mnemonic label.

If no switch is indicated (e.g., the mnemonic labeled SWOLH in the majors) then the item is interpreted as a finding which requires a positive response to a question to be asked during consultation. The switch "/F" is used to indicate that a negative response is required for a finding. The switch "/H" means that the item is an intermediate conclusion (hypothesis) and therefore rules are needed to conclude it (e.g., the mnemonic labeled RAYES in the major list is an intermediate conclusion). The switch "/N" indicates that the item is a finding that takes on a numeric value and the acceptable range is noted by a "RANGE" parameter. An example of a numeric finding is the item DCO with a valid range noted by (RANGE *:69) that means any numeric value less than 70.

The third section of the model is the diagnostic rules at the respective confidence levels of *Definite*, *Probable*, and *Possible*. The rules are grouped by confidence level where each rule is written using the mnemonic labels. It should be noted that logical conjunction is noted by the symbol "&" and disjunction is represented by having choices surrounded by the symbols "[" and "]". For example, one of the two rules at the probable confidence level indicates in its requirement component that at least one of three items noted by the mnemonics of MYOSS, RAYES, or DCO must be satisfied.

The fourth and last section of a tabular model in the structured editor format contains the rules for reaching intermediate conclusions that were referenced in the major and minor sections. An example is the first rule for concluding the major of *Raynaud's or esophogeal hypomotility* and is defined by the choice clause on the left-hand side of the arrow "->". The right-hand side specifies the mnemonic (i.e., RAYES) for the intermediate conclusion. Confidence for these intermediate rules may be specified by the numeric values which are allowed within the EXPERT formalism; the valid numeric values are in the range of -1 to 1 where -1 indicates complete denial of the conclusion and 1 indicates complete confirmation. By default, a confidence value of 1 is assumed when no confidence value is assigned on an intermediate rule.

This structured editor format of the model is translated into its equivalent EXPERT representation and is shown in the next section.

SEEK Editor-Format of Model

TABLE FOR DIAGNOSTIC CRITERIA

Mnemonic and English Description for DIAGNOSIS
MCTD   Mixed connective tissue disease

Mnemonic and English Description for MAJORS
RAYES/H Raynaud's or esophageal hypomotility
SWOLH   Swollen hands
SCLDY   Sclerodactyly
DCO/N   CO diff capacity, % nl: (RANGE *:69)
MYOSS/H Myositis, severe

Mnemonic and English Description for MINORS
ALOPE   Alopecia
WBC/N   WBC count, /cmm: (RANGE *:3999)
ANEM/H   Anemia - <=10 gm% female, <=12 gm% male
PLEUR   Pleuritis
PERIC   Pericarditis
ARTH   Arthritis <=6 wks, or non-polyarticular
MALAR   Malar (butterfly) rash
PLAT/N   Platelet count, /cmm (thousands): (RANGE *:99.99)
MYOSM/H Myositis, mild

Rules for DEFINITE confidence level

    # Majors: 4
    # Minors:
         Req: RNP & ENAVH/H
         Excl: SM

Rules for PROBABLE confidence level

    # Majors: 3
    # Minors:
         Req: RNP & ENAH/H
         Excl:

    # Majors: 2
    # Minors: 2
         Req: RNP & ENAH/H & [1: MYOSS/H, RAYES/H, DCO/N*:69]
         Excl:

Rules for POSSIBLE confidence level

    # Majors: 3
    # Minors:
         Req:
         Excl:

    # Majors: 2
    # Minors:
         Req: RNP & ENAM/H
         Excl:

    # Majors: 1
    # Minors: 3
         Req: RNP & ENAM/H
         Excl:

```
Rules for intermediate conclusions that are needed in diagnostic rules
RAYES    Raynaud's or esophageal hypomotility
[1: RAYN, ESOPH]  -> RAYES
ENAM     positive ENA, Med titer
[1: ENANP/N100:*, ENANH/N100:*]  -> ENAM
ENAH     positive ENA, Hi titer
[1: ENANP/N1000:*, ENANH/N1000:*]  -> ENAH
ENAVH    positive ENA, Very hi titer
[1: ENANP/N4000:*, ENANH/N4000:*]  -> ENAVH
MYOSM    Myositis, mild
AMEM & EMG  -> MYOSM
AMEM & [1: PMWM, MBXM]  -> MYOSM
MYOSS    Myositis, severe
AMES  -> MYOSS
PMWS  -> MYOSS
MYOSM/H & MBXS  -> MYOSS
ANEM     Anemia - <=10 gm% female, <=12 gm% male
HGB/N*:10 & FEM  -> ANEM
HGB/N*:12 & MALE  -> ANEM
```

II.3 EXPERT Format for a Model

This section shows the overall structure of an EXPERT model in which certain parts of the tabular model for MCTD are filled in. A valid EXPERT model description consists of three main sections: hypotheses, findings, and rules. Hypotheses for describing the conclusions that are to be reached during consultation are divided into two subsections to contain the final conclusions and intermediate conclusions. In this example, the final conclusion of MCTD is placed in the *TAXONOMY* subsection while intermediate conclusions such as RAYES are placed in the *CAUSAL and INTERMEDIATE* subsection.

The findings which are to be asked during consultation are placed in the ***FINDINGS* section of an EXPERT model. The findings in all models used by SEEK are organized into a questionnaire which the model designer prepares--this is shown below the ***FINDING* label.

The third section of an EXPERT model contains the rules. This is noted by the ***RULES* label that appears below the questionnaire. The rules for reaching all intermediate conclusions are included in order as they were specified in the SEEK editor; these rules for intermediate conclusions appear before the rules for the final diagnostic conclusions. The last group of rules that conclude MCTD are listed and include the rules for *possible* MCTD (noted by the .4 confidence values), *probable* MCTD (.7 confidence values), and *definite* MCTD (.9 confidence values).

```
**HYPOTHESES
*TAXONOMY
MCTD      Mixed connective tissue disease
  .
  .

*CAUSAL and INTERMEDIATE HYPOTHESES
RAYES     Raynaud's or esophageal hypomotility
ENAM      positive ENA, Med titer
ENAH      positive ENA, Hi titer
ENAVH     positive ENA, Very hi titer
MYOSM     Myositis, mild
MYOSS     Myositis, severe
ANEM      Anemia - <=10 gm% female, <=12 gm% male
MJMCT     Majors for MCTD
MNMCT     Minors for MCTD
RD102     Requirement 1 for Definite MCTD
ED102     Exclusion 1 for Definite MCTD
RR102     Requirement 1 for Probable MCTD
RR202     Requirement 2 for Probable MCTD
RS102     Requirement 1 for Possible MCTD

**FINDINGS
*begin questionnaire
*checklist
General Findings:
MALE      Patient is male
FEM       Patient is female
  .
  .

*checklist
Presumptive Diagnosis:
DXMCT     Mixed Connective Tissue Disease
DXRA      Rheumatoid Arthritis
DXSLE     Systemic Lupus Erythematosus
DXPSS     Progressive Systemic Sclerosis
DXPM      Polymyositis
DXPRA     Primary Raynaud's
DXSJ      Sjogren's
*end questionnaire

**RULES
  .
  .
  .

[1:F(RAYN,T),F(ESOPH,T)]->H(RAYES,1.)
[1:F(ENANP,100:*),F(ENANH,100:*)]->H(ENAM,1.)
[1:F(ENANP,1000:*),F(ENANH,1000:*)]->H(ENAH,1.)
[1:F(ENANP,4000:*),F(ENANH,4000:*)]->H(ENAVH,1.)
F(AMEM,T)&F(EMG,T)->H(MYOSM,1.)
F(AMEM,T)&[1:F(PMWM,T),F(MBXM,T)]->H(MYOSM,1.)
F(AMES,T)->H(MYOSS,1.)
F(PMWS,T)->H(MYOSS,1.)
H(MYOSM,.9:*)&F(MBXS,T)->H(MYOSS,1.)
F(HGB,*:10)&F(FEM,T)->H(ANEM,1.)
F(HGB,*:12)&F(MALE,T)->H(ANEM,1.)
```

180

```
/    Mixed connective tissue disease
[1:H(RAYES,.9:1.),F(SWOLH,T),F(SCLDY,T),F(DCO,*:69),H(MYOSS,.9:1.)]
   ->H(MJMCT,.1)
   .
   .
   .

[1:F(ALOPE,T),F(WBC,*:3999),H(ANEM,.9:1.),F(PLEUR,T),F(PERIC,T),
   F(ARTH,T),F(MALAR,T),F(PLAT,*:99.99),H(MYOSM,.9:1.)]->H(MNMCT,.1)
   .
   .
   .
F(RNP,T)&H(ENAVH,.9:*)->H(RD1O2,1.)
F(SM,T)->H(ED1O2,1.)
F(RNP,T)&H(ENAH,.9:*)&
   [1:H(MYOSS,.9:*),H(RAYES,.9:*),F(DCO,*:69)]->H(RR1O2,1.)
F(RNP,T)&H(ENAH,.9:*)->H(RR2O2,1.)
F(RNP,T)&H(ENAM,.9:*)->H(RS1O2,1.)
H(MJMCT,.1:*)&H(MNMCT,.3:*)&H(RS1O2,.9:*)->H(MCTD,.4)
H(MJMCT,.2:*)&H(RS1O2,.9:*)->H(MCTD,.4)
H(MJMCT,.3:*)->H(MCTD,.4)
H(MJMCT,.2:*)&H(MNMCT,.2:*)&H(RR1O2,.9:*)->H(MCTD,.7)
H(MJMCT,.3:*)&H(RR2O2,.9:*)->H(MCTD,.7)
H(MJMCT,.4:*)&H(RD1O2,.9:*)&H(ED1O2,-1.:.O5)->H(MCTD,.9)
*END RULES
```

REFERENCES

[1]   Aikins, J. S.
        Prototypes and Production Rules: An Approach to Knowledge Representation for
        Hypothesis Formation.
        In *Proceedings of the Sixth International Joint Conference on Artificial Intelligence*,
        pages 1-3.   Tokyo, Japan, 1979.

[2]   Aikins, J. S.
        *Prototypes and Production Rules: A Knowledge Representation for Computer
        Consultations.*
        Technical Report HPP-80-17, Heuristic Programming Project, Stanford University,
        1980.
        Ph.D. Thesis.

[3]   Balzer, R., Erman, L., London, P., Williams, C.
        A Domain-Independent Framework for Expert Systems.
        In *Proceedings of the First National Conference on Artificial Intelligence*, pages
        108-110.   1980.

[4]   Bennett, James S. and Engelmore, Robert S.
        SACON: A Knowledge-Based Consultant for Structural Analysis.
        In *Proceedings of the Sixth International Joint Conference on Artificial Intelligence*,
        pages 47-49.   Tokyo, Japan, 1979.

[5]   Buchanan, B. G. and Mitchell, T. M.
        Model-directed learning of production rules.
        In D. A. Waterman and F. Hayes-Roth (editor), *Pattern-Directed Inference Systems*.
        Academic Press, New York, 1978.

[6]   Davis, R.
        Interactive Transfer of Expertise: Acquisition of New Inference Rules.
        In *Proceedings of the Fifth International Joint Conference on Artificial Intelligence*,
        pages 321-328.   August, 1977.

[7]   Dieterich, T. G. and Michalski, R. S.
        Learning and Generalization of Characteristic Descriptions: Evaluation Criteria and
        Comparative Review of Selected Methods.
        In *Proceedings of the Sixth International Joint Conference on Artificial Intelligence*.
        Tokyo, Japan, 1979.

[8]   Duda, R. O. and Hart, P. E.
        Pattern Classification and Scene Analysis.
        Wiley, New York, 1973.

[9]   Forgy, C., and J. McDermott.
        OPS, A Domain-Independent production system language.
        In *Proceedings of the Fifth International Joint Conference on Artificial Intelligence*,
        pages 933-939.   1977.

[10]   Friedland, P.
       Acquisition of Procedural Knowledge from Domain Experts.
       In *Proceedings of the Seventh International Joint Conference on Artificial
           Intelligence*, pages 856-861. 1981.

[11]   Fries, J. F.
       Time-Oriented Patient Records and a Computer Data Bank.
       Journal of American Medical Association 222:1536-1542, 1972.

[12]   Fries, J. F.
       A Data Bank for the Clinician?
       New England Journal of Medicine 294:1400-1402, 1976.

[13]   Fukunaga, K.
       Introduction to Statistical Pattern Recognition.
       Academic Press, New York, 1972.

[14]   Gaschnig, J.
       Preliminary Performance Analysis of the Prospector Consultant System for Mineral
           Exploration.
       In *Proceedings of the Sixth International Joint Conference on Artificial Intelligence*,
           pages 308-310. Tokyo, Japan, 1979.

[15]   Gaschnig, J.
       An Application of the Prospector System to DOE's National Uranium Resource
           Evaluation.
       In *Proceedings of the First National Conference on Artificial Intelligence*, pages
           295-297. Stanford, California, 1980.

[16]   Ginsberg, A., Weiss, S., and Politakis, P.
       An Overview of the SEEK2 Project.
       Technical Report, Department of Computer Science, Rutgers University, 1985.

[17]   Gorry, G. A.
       Computer-assisted Clinical Decision-making.
       Methods Inform. Med. 12:45-51, 1973.

[18]   Kulikowski, C. A.
       Artificial Intelligence Methods and Systems for Medical Consultation.
       IEEE Transactions on Pattern Analysis and Machine Intelligence PAMI-2(5):464-476,
           September, 1980.

[19]   Ledley, R. S. and Lusted, L. B.
       Reasoning Foundation of Medical Diagnosis: Symbolic Logic, Probability and Value
           Theory Aid Our Understanding of How Physicians Reason.
       Science 130:9-21, 1959.

[20]   Lenat, D. B.
       Automated Theory Formation in Mathematics.
       In *Proceedings of the Fifth International Joint Conference on Artificial Intelligence*,
           pages 833-842. MIT, Cambridge, MA, August, 1977.

[21]   Lenat, D. B.
       EURISKO: Discovery of Heuristics by Heuristic Search.
       Technical Report, Heuristic Programming Project, Stanford University, Stanford,
           California, 1982.
       Working Paper.

[22]   Lenat, D. B.
       Heuretics: Theoretical and Experimental Study of Heuristic Rules.
       In *Proceedings of the Second National Conference on Artificial Intelligence,* pages
           159-163. 1982.

[23]   Lichter, Paul R., Anderson, Douglas R.
       Discussions on Glaucoma.
       Grune and Stratton, New York, 1977.

[24]   Lindberg, D., Sharp, G., Kingsland, L., Weiss, S., Hayes, S., Ueno, H.,Hazelwood, S.
       Computer Based Rheumatology Consultant.
       In *Proceedings of the Third World Conference on Medical Informatics,* pages
           1311-1315. 1980.

[25]   Michalski, R. S.
       AQVAL/1 - Computer implementation of a variable valued logic system VL1 and
           examples of its application to pattern recognition.
       In *Procedings 1st International Joint Conference on Pattern Recognition,* pages 3-17.
           Washington, D. C., 1973.

[26]   Mitchell, T. M.
       Version Spaces: A candidate elimination approach to rule learning.
       In *Proceedings of the Fifth International Joint Conference on Artificial Intelligence,*
           pages 305-310. MIT, Cambridge, Mass., August, 1977.

[27]   Mitchell, Tom.
       Generalization as Search.
       Artificial Intelligence :203-226, 1982.

[28]   Nii, H. P. and Aiello, N.
       AGE (Attempt to Generalize): A Knowledge-based Program for Building Knowledge-
           Based Programs.
       In *Proceedings of the Sixth International Joint Conference on Artificial Intelligence,*
           pages 645-655. 1979.

[29]   Nilsson, N. J.
       Learning Machines.
       McGraw-Hill, New York, 1965.

[30]   Pauker, S., Gorry, G., Kassirer, J., Schwartz, W.
       Toward the Simulation of Clinical Cognition: Taking the Present Illness by
           Computer.
       American Journal of Medicine 60:981-995, 1976.

[31]   Politakis, P. and S. Weiss.
       *Designing Consistent Knowledge Bases: An Approach to Expert Knowledge
           Acquisition.*
       Technical Report CBM-TR-113, LCSR Rutgers University, 1980.

[32]   Politakis, P. and S.M. Weiss.
         Using Empirical Analysis to Refine Expert System Knowledge Bases.
         Artificial Intelligence 22:23-48, 1984.

[33]   Pople, H., Myers, J., and Miller, R.
         DIALOG: A Model of Diagnostic Logic for Internal Medicine.
         In *Proceedings of the Fourth International Joint Conference on Artificial Intelligence*,
             pages 841-846. 1975.

[34]   Reboh, R.
         Knowledge Engineering Techniques and Tools in the Prospector Environment.
         Technical Report Technical Note 243, SRI International, 1981.

[35]   Samuel, A. L.
         Some studies in machine learning using the game of checkers.
         In E. A. Feigenbaum and J. Feldman (editor), *Computers and Thought*, pages 71-105.
             McGraw-Hill, New York, 1963.

[36]   Shortliffe, Edward Hance.
         Computer-Based Medical Consultations: MYCIN.
         Elsevier Scientific Publishing Company, Inc., New York, 1976.
         Adaptation of Doctoral Thesis.

[37]   Smith, R. G., et al.
         A model for learning systems.
         In *Proceedings of the Fifth International Joint Conference on Artificial Intelligence*,
             pages 338-343. Cambridge, MA, 1977.

[38]   Stallman, R.
         EMACS Manual for Twenex Users
         MIT, 1980.
         AI MEMO 554.

[39]   Stefik, M. J.
         An Examination of a Frame-Structured Representation Scheme.
         In *Proceedings of the Sixth International Joint Conference on Artificial Intelligence*,
             pages 845-852. 1979.

[40]   Stefik, M. J.
         Planning with Constraints.
         PhD thesis, Stanford University, January, 1980.

[41]   Szolovits, P., and S. Pauker.
         Categorical and Probabilistic Reasoning in Medical Diagnosis.
         Artificial Intelligence 11:115-144, 1978.

[42]   Van Melle, W.
         A domain-independent production-rule system for consultation programs.
         In *Proceedings of the Sixth International Joint Conference on Artificial Intelligence*,
             pages 923-925. Tokyo, Japan, 1979.

[43]   Vanker, A.D., W. Van Stoecker.
         An Expert Diagnostic Program for Dermatology.
         Computers and Biomedical Research 17:241-247, 1984.

[44]   Warner, H. R., Toronto, A. F., and Veasy, L. G.
       Experience with Bayes Theorem for Computer Diagnosis of Congenital Heart Disease.
       Annals New York Acad. Sciences 115:558-567, 1964.

[45]   Waterman, D. A.
       Generalization learning techniques for automating the learning of heuristics.
       Artificial Intelligence 1(1,2):121-170, 1970.

[46]   Weiss, S. and C. Kulikowski.
       The EXPERT and CASNET Consultation Systems.
       In *Proceedings Japan-AIM Workshop.* Tokyo, August, 1979.

[47]   Weiss, S., Kulikowski, C., and Safir, A.
       Glaucoma Consultation by Computer.
       Computers in Biology and Medicine (1):25-40, 1978.

[48]   Weiss, S., Kulikowski, C. and Nudel, B.
       Learning Production Rules for Consultation Systems.
       In *Proceedings of the Sixth International Joint Conference on Artificial Intelligence*,
           pages 948-950. Tokyo, August, 1979.

[49]   S. Weiss and C. Kulikowski.
       EXPERT: A System for Developing Consultation Models.
       Technical Report CBM-TR-97, Rutgers University, January, 1979.

[50]   Weiss, S., Kulikowski, C., Galen, R.
       Developing Microprocessor Based Expert Models for Instrument Interpretation.
       In *Proceedings of the Seventh International Joint Conference on Artificial
           Intelligence*, pages 853-855. Vancouver, Canada, 1981.

[51]   Weiss, S. M., Kern, K. B., Kulikowski, C. A., Uschold, M. F.
       A Guide to the Use of the EXPERT Consultation System.
       Technical Report, Rutgers University, May, 1981.
       CBM-TR-94.

[52]   Winston, P. H. (editor).
       The Psychology of Computer Vision.
       McGraw-Hill, New York, 1975.

[53]   Yu, V., et al.
       Evaluating the Performance of a Computer-Based Consultant.
       Technical Report HPP-78-17, Heuristic Programming Project, Stanford University,
           1978.